ANCIENT
TREES

Trees That Live For 1000 Years

ANCIENT TREES

TREES

Trees That Live For 1000 Years

Anna Lewington & Edward Parker

To Eppie and Aaron

First published in Great Britain in 1999 by
Collins & Brown Limited
London House
Great Eastern Wharf
Parkgate Road
London SW11 4NQ

Distributed in the United States and Canada by Sterling Publishing Co,
387 Park Avenue South, New York, NY 10016, USA

1 3 5 7 9 8 6 4 2

British Library Cataloguing-in-Publication Data:
A catalogue record for this title is available from the British Library.

ISBN 1-85585-704-9 (hardback)
ISBN 1-85585-754-5 (paperback)

Editorial Director: Sarah Hoggett
Editors: Katie Bent and Mandy Greenfield
Design Manager: Alison Lee
Original Design Concept: Roger Daniels
Jacket Design: Alison Lee

Reproduced by Hong Kong Graphic and Printing
Printed and bound by Imago, Hong Kong

CONTENTS

INTRODUCTION

'Among all the varied productions with which Nature has adorned the surface of the earth, none awakens our sympathies, or interests our imagination so powerfully as those venerable trees which seem to have stood the lapse of ages, silent witnesses of the successive generations of man, to whose destiny they bear so touching a resemblance, alike in their budding, their prime and their decay.'

JOHN MUIR, 1868

BELOW

Many ancient trees have had to adapt to environmental challenges. This yew has spread its roots over bare rock.

THE RESEARCH FOR THIS BOOK HAS TAKEN us on a journey of discovery, not just around the world, but also through time. We have encountered giants whose enormous fluted trunks rise up like great cathedrals, and we have stood in groves of gnarled and wizened trees that were alive before the great pyramids of ancient Egypt were built, standing in a desolate landscape that has remained virtually unchanged for 20,000 years. We have sensed the quiet power of some of the world's largest and oldest living organisms, and begun to understand the awe and reverence that many peoples in the past have felt. Standing in the presence of some of the world's oldest statesmen, it was impossible not to feel moved and reflect upon the transience of our own human lives; impossible not to feel that we are part of natural cycles that are just too large for us to comprehend.

At the very beginning of this project we were hoping to include some twenty-four species of trees that live to over 1,000 years. As our research progressed, however, we discovered more and more examples of ancient trees from all round the world. The number of candidates has now risen to nearly 100 species, and the list is still growing. We were intrigued to find that ancient trees occur on all the continents of the globe, with the exception of Antarctica, and that many are easily accessible to millions of people – rural and urban alike. There are 1,000-year-old trees in the Chinese capital, Beijing; within a four-hour drive of Los Angeles; on the outskirts of London; and even close to the largest city in the Amazon rain forest, Manaus. It is pleasing to know that 1,000-year-old trees are widely enough scattered for many of us to enjoy and visit them easily.

As we prepare to enter the third millennium since the birth of Christ, some of the world's oldest and most impressive inhabitants have already begun their fourth, fifth, sixth or even seventh millennium. In the White Mountains of California some bristlecone pines (*Pinus longaeva*) are approaching 5,000 years old, while a number of Europe's venerable olive trees (*Olea europaea*) were almost certainly growing at the time of Christ. And the great forests of cedar of Lebanon (*Cedrus libani*) provided the timber to build King Solomon's temple in the tenth century BC. In woodland in the west of England, however, a small-leaved lime (*Tilia cordata*) has already celebrated its 6,000th birthday, while the common yew (*Taxus baccata*) growing at Fortingall in Scotland may be an astonishing 9,000 years old.

THE LONGEVITY OF TREES

No one knows which living tree is currently the oldest in the world or how many tree species produce individuals that live to over 1,000 years.

ABOVE
A mighty baobab rises out of the savannah in South Africa's Kruger National Park.

Attempting to age trees accurately is, as the retired British forest-research dendrologist John White has put it, 'a new science'. It is therefore possible to speculate wildly on the ages of individual trees in the absence of hard evidence. The French botanist Michel Adanson (1727–1806), who gave his name to the mighty baobabs (*Adansonia* sp.), enraged the world when he estimated the age of a giant African tree at 6,000 years old, leading to a questioning of the date of the biblical flood. It appears today, however, that his calculations may not have been that far awry.

What we can say with certainty is that the world's most ancient trees occur in a wide variety of environments around the world, from the temperate climates of England and New Zealand to the intense tropical heat of the Amazon rain forest. For some tree species such as the bristlecone pine, harsh environmental conditions (such as intense cold, high altitude and drought) seem actually to encourage the attainment of great age.

We have also observed that trees can reach ages of over 1,000 years in a variety of ways. In some instances this appears to be related to local environmental conditions; in others it is, fascinatingly, due directly to the intervention of humans. Trees in this category include the olive (*Olea europaea*), sweet chestnut (*Castanea sativa*), oaks (*Quercus* spp.) and limes (*Tilia* spp.), which have regularly been coppiced or pollarded over long periods of time. Another example of the fruit of human intervention is the famous bo tree (*Ficus religiosa*) at Anuradhapura on the island of Sri Lanka, which was planted in a temple garden in 288 BC and has been carefully tended ever since.

There are several contenders for the world's longest-lived tree species, and perhaps all that most scientists will agree on is that great overestimates have been made

concerning the ages of some. Interestingly, many of the candidates are conifers and include the common yew, the bristlecone pine and – beyond the scope of this book – the Japanese cedar (*Cryptomeria japonica*) and the huon pine (*Dacrydium franklinii*). In addition, various shrubs are extremely long-lived (perhaps even more so than trees), including the creosote bush (*Larrea* sp.) from California's Mojave Desert (over 11,000 years old) and the king's holly (*Lomatia tasmanica*) from Tasmania.

The problem with identifying the world's oldest trees is that there is no single fool-proof way to calculate the age of many of the most ancient individuals. The most common methods are by counting annual tree rings and by radiocarbon-dating material taken from the oldest part of the tree. However, both these methods involve damaging the tree to some extent in order to take a sample of material for analysis. In addition, many trees

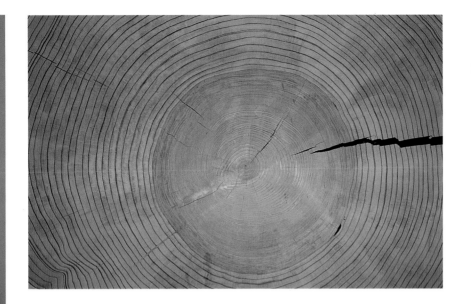

LEFT
―――
*Trees with clearly visible growth rings,
like this coast redwood, can generally be
aged accurately.*

become hollow as they get older, making both methods redundant. Even the relatively simple method of counting tree rings is not as straightforward as it might appear because some trees do not produce rings evenly – or at all – in some years, or under certain conditions. Some trees, such as the common yew, appear to stop growing at certain stages of their lives (or certain parts of the tree stop growing) and then begin to grow again, giving partial and irregular ring sequences in areas of the tree.

A number of tree experts around the world, such as John White, are now refining techniques to develop new methodologies that can be used to estimate the age of certain trees. The method used by White involves measuring the girth of the tree trunk at a consistent height from the ground (normally 4¼ ft/1.3 m) and comparing its size to that of other tree trunks in similar sites, some of which may already have been cut down. Then, using information gathered about growth rates from many examples of a particular tree species, it is possible to create a model that reflects the rate of increase in diameter during the usual three distinct growth phases of the tree. Recently it has been shown that, contrary to earlier assumptions, tree rings laid down over a long period of time are not uniform in size, and in old age the rings can become very small, or even absent in bad growing years. This dating method is accurate where there is a wealth of tree-ring data about a particular tree, but inappropriate for ageing relatively unknown species.

New discoveries are surprising botanists all the time – only recently, for instance, has it been discovered, by means of radiocarbon-dating the trunks of felled trees, that there are at least four Amazonian species that can live to well over 1,000 years: the castanha de macaco (*Cariniana micrantha*), cumaru (*Dipteryx odorata*), angelim da mata (*Hymenolobium* spp.) and the maçaranduba (*Manilkara huberi*).

The discovery of the Wollemi pine (*Wollemia nobilis*) in a deep gorge near Sydney astounded botanists. The oldest individual is calculated to be well over 1,000 years old and the trees closely resemble fossils of an extinct genus of the Araucariacae family, that may date back in origin at least 100 million years. According to Carrick Chambers, the Director of Sydney's Royal Botanic Gardens, the discovery was like 'finding a small dinosaur still alive on earth'. Because of its ability to clone itself by coppicing it could turn out to be one of the longest-lived species on the planet.

Fascinating though this debate is, this book is not designed to identify the world's oldest individual tree or to be a definitive guide to all the world's ancient trees. Rather, it is a celebration of certain tree species and groups of trees containing individuals that will be at least 1,000 years old at the beginning of the millennium.

OBJECTS OF RESPECT

Since the earliest times trees have had a special fascination for humankind. Across large areas of the world where now only scattered remnants remain, vast forests once stretched unbroken. These forests, the original wildwoods, provided our ancestors with shelter and food, medicines and other necessities, but many of the trees also represented something more. As the biggest and most invincible of all living things, they must have helped shape the consciousness of people (not just meet their practical needs), as they tried to make sense of their world.

It is not difficult to imagine how, with their huge trunks reaching upwards from their anchors in the earth and their branches seeming to touch the sky, some of the world's giant and most ancient trees – whose lifespans far exceeded those of human beings – should have seemed immortal and come to occupy a special place within the greater scheme of things; to appear in some way connected with the forces governing the earth, and to be able to directly influence peoples' lives.

Around the world many large and slow-growing individual trees have been – and still are for many people today – the objects of deep respect, and often a religious reverence, making them sacred and setting them apart from other trees. Such feelings appear to have distinguished one of, if not indeed the longest-lived of Europe's tree species, the common yew in the distant past. This tree's mysterious ability to continue to renew itself from a state of apparent decay, and its deadly poisonous but evergreen leaves, helped to confer upon it the status of immortality and place it at the centre of a sacred cult associated with the after-life. The most common signs of this remain in evidence today in the wealth of ancient yews that still create a deeply mystical aura in churchyards throughout northern Europe.

The great European oaks (*Quercus robur* and *Q. petraea*) and the limes (chiefly *Tilia cordata* and *T. platyphyllos*) also came to acquire a sacred status of their own – the former being associated with the Norse and Germanic gods of thunder and lightning, and the limes with fertility. Sacrifices were made to the powerful supernatural beings associated with these trees, in the hope of influencing the lives of people on earth. The Celts are a well-known example of a European people whose lives were dominated by trees and the forces they were believed to represent. Describing their tendency to create sacred groves or sanctuaries in forest clearings or glades, the Roman historian Gaius Cornelius Tacitus (AD *c.* 55–120) wrote of the Celts living beyond the Roman empire:

'They deem it incompatible with the majesty of the heavenly host to confine the gods within walls, or to mould them into any likeness of the human face; they consecrate groves and coppices, and they give the divine names to that mysterious something which is visible only to the eyes of faith.'

Such beliefs in the sacred powers or mystical forces of trees are still strongly present in many urban societies today, and are only superficially hidden from view. The most familiar Western good-luck charm of 'touching wood', for example, is, according to Jacqueline Memory Paterson, the author of *Tree Wisdom*:

'a direct continuation of the actions of our Celtic ancestors, who at times of need went to certain trees and touched and communed with them. These trees were thought to contain or house specific spirits, such as those associated with the elements and gods and goddesses.'

To many of the world's ethnic groups today, who have been able to maintain their cultural traditions (at least in part), trees continue to provide both a practical and a spiritual focus to their lives. One such example

The 1,100-year-old ginkgo at Yon Mun temple near Seoul in South Korea, displaying brilliant yellow foliage.

are the Pehuenche Indians of south-central Chile, whose name and identity have been determined by the monkey puzzle trees (*Araucaria araucana*) among which they have traditionally lived. Pehuenche means 'people of the monkey puzzle tree', for the tree is sacred to them, and their diet is still based upon the nutritious seeds produced by the trees. These are able to live to an estimated 2,000 years, and once covered a much larger area of the southern hemisphere. The Pehuenche have been battling for years to save their ancestral forests from international logging concerns, but with only limited success.

On the North American continent the continued commercial felling of Douglas firs (*Pseudotsuga menziesii*) – some of which were even taller than the coast redwoods (*Sequoia sempervirens*) and possibly older than the giant redwoods (*Sequoiadendron giganteum*) – has been the cause of much public concern. This is also true of the continued felling of the coast redwoods, which were once important to a number of North American indigenous tribes, leading to considerable protest. For many people it is difficult to understand why the destruction of these fantastic ancient trees should continue, especially as the coast redwood forests have already been reduced to just 5 per cent of their original area. Fortunately, some of the best coast redwood forest has recently been saved from clear felling, after a battle that has lasted ten years and cost the life of at least one protester.

Elsewhere, the traditional reverence that has characterized the relationship of entire peoples with certain trees continues to offer them some protection. In India, for example, the banyan fig (*Ficus benghalensis*) is protected not only because it has long been considered a sacred tree, but because its shade is greatly valued. Strict regulations control the usage or treatment of banyans, for religious and practical reasons: some, situated along routes regularly traversed by people on elephants, are reserved for fodder. Similar beliefs are held about the bodhi tree (*Ficus religiosa*), the sacred fig of India, Sri Lanka and parts of Southeast Asia, beneath which Buddha is believed to have attained enlightenment, and thus the most sacred of all trees to Buddhists; and about the remarkable ginkgo (*Ginkgo biloba*) in China and Korea, which – though almost extinct in the wild – continues to thrive in temple gardens, where it was traditionally planted by Buddhist and other monks.

The remarkable secular uses to which people around the world have put their age-old trees is well illustrated by the baobab and boab trees of Africa and Australia. Here, the hollow trunks of ancient trees have been variously used as prisons, store rooms, lavatories and even pubs! Despite such usage, and though it cannot be beneficial to the longevity of the trees, they have been able to survive.

LITERARY AND ARTISTIC INSPIRATION
Ancient trees have been a constant source of inspiration to poets, artists and storytellers throughout the ages. William Wordsworth (1770–1850), for instance, drew inspiration from ancient yew trees in 'The Pride of Lorton Vale' and 'The Fraternal Four'. For Vincent Van Gogh (1853–90) the subtleties of colour and texture of the olive trees of Provence inspired and drove him to distraction in almost equal measure. Thomas Jefferson (1743–1826) was inspired to write, 'The olive tree is surely the richest gift from

heaven', while Aldous Huxley (1894–1963) recorded his feelings as follows: 'I like them all, but especially the olive. For what it symbolizes, first of all – peace with its leaves and joy with its golden oil.' And William Blake's passion for trees was summed up in one of his works, published in 1799, which read:

'The tree that moves some to tears of joy is in the eyes of others only a green thing that stands in the way. Some see Nature all Ridicule and Deformity … and some scarce see Nature at all. But to the eyes of the Man of Imagination, Nature is Imagination itself.'

All round the world ancient trees feature in oral traditions, with myths and legends – such as the Maori story of 'The Kauri and the Whale' (see p. 143) – often being retold with an innate poetic grace and subtle metre.

OUR ANCIENT LIVING HERITAGE

Whatever the experts may decide about the exact ages of our oldest trees, and despite the continued excesses of logging companies in some parts of the world, a resurgence of interest in saving and appreciating our ancient living heritage has recently become apparent among people from all walks of life.

In Britain – which can proudly boast more old and ancient trees than anywhere else in northwest Europe – various initiatives have captured the popular mood. While the Tree Register of the British Isles is busily documenting and building an accurate database of the nation's record trees, other projects have also come to the fore, such as the Veteran Tree Initiative – veteran trees being those that 'because of their great age, size or condition are of exceptional value culturally in the landscape or for wildlife'. This initiative aims to 'promote the conservation of Veteran Trees wherever they occur to ensure their future continuity'. Many trees are also being planted to celebrate the new millennium.

Ordinary people all round the world, from Chile to Bhutan, are now fighting to save their forests. On an international level the World Wildlife Fund's 'Forests For Life' initiative is actively campaigning for the protection of natural forests worldwide. It has persuaded many governments, from Brazil to Thailand, to protect large areas of forest in order to help conserve global biodiversity, and to continue to provide valuable environmental services, such as flood protection, carbon-dioxide sequestration and local climate regulation. The Forests For Life campaign has supported this book from its inception.

As the second millennium draws to a close, we are in many ways rediscovering our common link with our ancient ancestors through a new respect and reverence for forests and, in particular, venerable old trees. And in a world increasingly dominated by change, these ancient veterans provide a tangible link with our past, serving to remind us of the extraordinary antiquity and beauty of life on earth. This book is intended to be a celebration of some of the world's most ancient trees.

OPPOSITE

Today only small remnants of the once vast cedar of Lebanon forests remain, reminding us of our duty to protect such ancient treasures.

ANCIENT TREES OF THE WORLD

KEY

1. **Coast redwood:** California, USA.
2. **Giant redwood:** California, USA.
3. **Dawn redwood:** Hubei Province, China
4. **Bristlecone pine:** White Mountains of California, Nevada and Utah, USA.
5. **Montezuma cypress:** Mexico.
6. **Monkey puzzle:** found in the Cordillera of the Andes, along the borders of Chile and Argentina.
7. **Brazil nut:** widespread across the Amazon basin.
8. **Castanha de macao:** Amazon rain forest, Brazil.
9. **Cumaru:** Amazon rain forest, Brazil.
10. **Angelim da mata:** Amazon rain forest, Brazil.
11. **Maçaranduba:** Amazon rain forest, Brazil.
12. **Yew:** oldest – Fortingall yew, Scotland. Species widely distributed across Europe, North Africa and West Asia.
13. **Oak:** Bowthorpe oak, England. Species distributed across Europe and the coast of western North Africa.
14. **Oak:** oldest – Nordskoven Forest, Denmark.
15. **Sweet chestnut:** Tree of a Hundred Horses, Sicily. Species distributed across southern Europe, western Asia and North Africa.

16. **Small-leaved lime:** oldest – Westonbirt Arboretum, England. Species found across Europe to Siberia and Asia Minor.
17. **Broad-leaved lime:** The Tassillo Lime, near Munich, Bavaria. Species found across Europe to Siberia and Asia Minor.
18. **Olive:** Garden of Gethsemane, Jerusalem, Israel. Species widespread across the Mediterranean.
19. **Welwitschia:** Found on northern plains of the Namib Desert, from the Kuiseb River to southern Angola.
20. **Baobab:** largest – Sagole, Northern Province, South Africa. Species widespread across most of the African continent.
21. **Madagascan baobabs:** Madagascar.
22. **Baobab:** The Prison Tree, Derby, Western Australia.
23. **Kauri:** largest surviving – Tane Mahuta, Waipoua Forest, North Island. Species found on Northern North Island, New Zealand.
24. **Totara:** oldest surviving – Pureora mountains near Taupo, North Island, New Zealand. Species found on North and South Islands, New Zealand.

25. **Antarctic Beech:** Southeastern Queensland and northeastern New South Wales, Australia.

26. **Banyan fig:** largest – Bombay, India. Species found in all tropical and some temperate regions.

27. **Bodhi fig:** oldest – Anuradhapura, southeastern Sri Lanka. Species found in all tropical and some temperate regions.

28. **Bodhi fig:** famous 'Bodhi Tree', Bihar, India.

29. **Sycamore fig:** largest – Kruger National Park, South Africa. Species found in all tropical and some temperate regions.

30. **Atlas cedar:** Atlas Mountains of Algeria and Morocco.

31. **Cedar of Cyprus:** Troodos Mountains, Cyprus.

32. **Cedar of Lebanon:** oldest – Bcharré Valley, Lebanon. Species found in Syria and Taurus Mountains, Turkey.

33. **Deodar:** Western Himalayas, from northern Pakistan and Afghanistan through Kashmir to western Nepal.

34. **Ginkgo:** Emperor's trees, Beijing, China. Some ancient trees found in mountains between Shejiang and Anhui provinces, China. Species widely cultivated.

35. **Gingko:** tallest – Yong Mun Sa temple, South Korea.

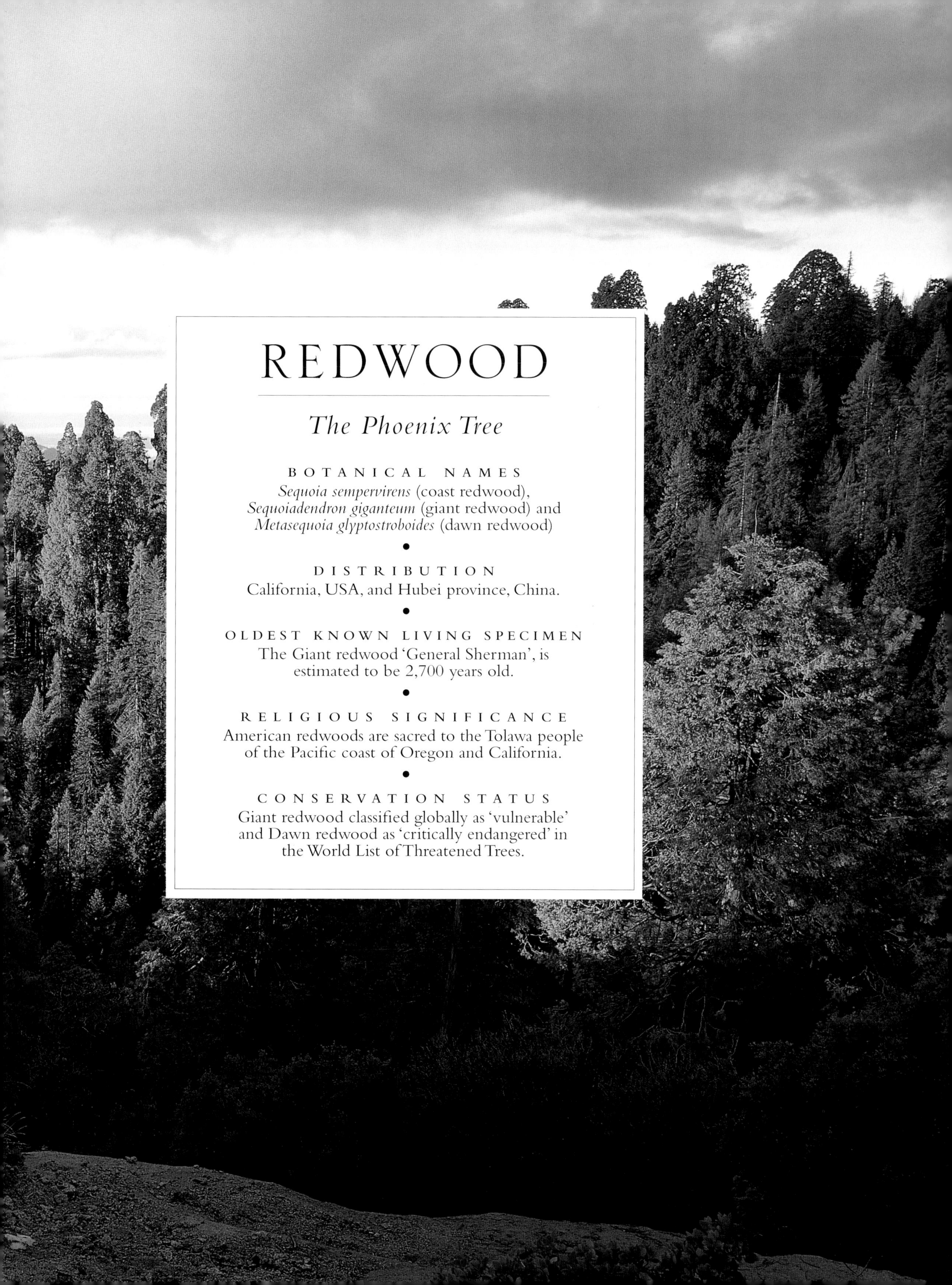

REDWOOD

The Phoenix Tree

BOTANICAL NAMES
Sequoia sempervirens (coast redwood),
Sequoiadendron giganteum (giant redwood) and
Metasequoia glyptostroboides (dawn redwood)

•

DISTRIBUTION
California, USA, and Hubei province, China.

•

OLDEST KNOWN LIVING SPECIMEN
The Giant redwood 'General Sherman', is
estimated to be 2,700 years old.

•

RELIGIOUS SIGNIFICANCE
American redwoods are sacred to the Tolawa people
of the Pacific coast of Oregon and California.

•

CONSERVATION STATUS
Giant redwood classified globally as 'vulnerable'
and Dawn redwood as 'critically endangered' in
the World List of Threatened Trees.

IMAGINE STANDING IN A FOREST of giants, believing that every living thing has a spirit. Imagine looking up at the elegant spires of the coast redwood trees, with their uppermost branches wreathed in mist, towering to over 300 ft/91 m above you. Imagine believing that every living thing was made by the supreme creator under the First Redwood Tree, and that redwoods are the guardians of the streams that provide the food on which you depend – the guardians of your very culture. For most of us it may be difficult to appreciate fully the reverence felt by indigenous peoples among these stately giants, but for the Tolawa people of the Pacific coast of California and Oregon such an awareness shaped their world for thousands of years before the arrival of Europeans.

The coast redwood (*Sequoia sempervirens*) which grows today along the Pacific coast of California, is a survivor from the forests that covered much of the northern hemisphere 140 million years ago. It is one of three surviving redwood species that retreated to small isolated areas with specific climatic conditions as the global climate changed. The giant sequoia or redwood (*Sequoiadendron giganteum*) is now restricted to the Sierra Nevada's western slopes in California, while the dawn redwood (*Metasequoia glyptostroboides*) is found only in a remote area of China.

BELOW

A view of part of the Redwood National Park on the Pacific coast of northern California.

THE COAST REDWOODS

The coast redwoods are graceful giants. Able to attain heights of over 300 ft/91 m, they are slim and elegant. Today the world's tallest living tree is a coast redwood known as 'Tall Tree', which stands in the Redwood National Park in northern California. Its age is estimated at over 1,500 years, and in 1990 it was 368 ft/112 m tall.

The coast redwood forests are located in a discontinuous belt that runs for 500 miles/805 km along the coasts of northern California and southern Oregon. They are rarely found far from the sea, the

furthest stand being just 30 miles/48 km inland, in Napa county. Much of the great redwood forest has now been logged and, despite vociferous protest, logging of large and ancient trees continues today.

Coast redwoods grow best in areas that have a mild climate and are protected from wind and salt spray. The tallest grow on the flood-plains of streams and rivers that are subject to periodic flooding. However, it is the high rainfall – more than 70 in/178 cm per year – and summer fogs that have allowed the redwoods to survive for so long in their refuge. The fog plays a particularly important role. It enables the trees to grow tall because the moisture that it carries condenses on their uppermost branches. As a result the redwoods do not have to conduct water all the way up the trunk from their roots.

Natural fires are also an important factor in the survival of these last remaining coast redwood forests. Redwood seeds have very specific requirements for germination: to be viable they need to be able to reach bare mineral soils, and the fires assist this process by burning away fallen needles and other organic material covering the soil, producing

A B O V E

The base of the elegant trunk of 'Tall Tree', the world's tallest coast redwood, at 368 ft/112 m high.

an ash that is rich in nutrients. Research has shown that, before the intervention of man, fires occurred every 20–50 years in the redwood forests, due to lightning strikes, which are a common occurrence in the Sierra Nevada.

The coast redwood has a thick, spongy bark that ranges in colour from reddish-brown to grey. The bark of mature trees may be 6–12 in/15–30 cm thick, and its high tannin content makes it resistant to both fire and attacks by fungi and insects.

The redwoods are conifers – that is, cone-bearing trees. The mature cones they produce are reddish-brown in colour, woody and very small. The seeds inside are minute flakes, which drift easily on a light wind, enabling them to disperse. In fact the seeds are so light that 125,000 of them weigh just 1 lb/0.45 kg. The coast redwoods have a second means of reproduction, by sprouting, or putting out suckers. They are the only cone-bearing trees able to do this.

In their coastal position, the redwoods protect the watersheds of many of the streams and rivers that are important as migratory routes and spawning grounds for salmon and sea trout. The rivers running through mature forest are crystal clear and provide ideal aquatic habitats; where the forests have been removed, the rivers become silted up with soil washed off the denuded slopes.

The role played by the coast redwood forests in the productivity of the rivers was long appreciated by the native peoples who lived – and in some places still live – along the Pacific coast. Before the 'discovery' of North America by Europeans, many different peoples with distinct languages, but a common culture, inhabited the forested coastlines of California and Oregon. Their societies were based on fishing, hunting and collecting forest produce. The redwoods provided continuity in a dynamic environment – even after catastrophic fires, they would be still standing, protecting the life-giving streams that teemed with fish.

Native peoples along the Pacific coast believed (and still do) that they are an inextricable part of nature, and that respect must be shown to all living things: both plants and animals. For example, whenever plants were gathered, the Kashaya Pomo people, who occupied the land in what is now Sonoma county (just north of San Francisco), offered a prayer to their supreme creator, explaining why these plants were being taken. A special song was sung to the 'earth spirit' to ward off evil; some form of personal sacrifice was also made – perhaps an offering of food or sharing of the produce collected. Selfishness was considered undesirable social behaviour, eventually leading to personal loss or bad luck.

Only 150 years ago the redwood forest along the Pacific coast was the home of numerous native peoples, including the Sinkyone, the Kashaya Pomo, the southwestern

The majestic sequoia is here, too, the King of Conifers, the noblest of all the noble race … these colossal trees are as wonderful in fineness of beauty and proportion as in stature – an assemblage of conifers surpassing all that have ever yet been discovered in the forests of the world.

JOHN MUIR

In the beginning there was nothing except water and darkness. Then the creator thought the world into existence. At the centre of the world stood the First Redwood Tree, beneath which were visible the tracks of all animals, which the creator had also thought into existence. These were pre-humans, which became rocks, trees and animals, and went away when the first people arrived.

THE TOLAWA CREATION MYTH

Pomo, the Wappo (Ashochimi), the Mendocino and the Tolawa. The Sinkyone people, who are extinct today, regarded the redwoods as sacred protectors of the whole forest, especially of the streams, on which so much else depended. Redwood groves acted as guardians of the spirits of their ancestors, whose sacred burial grounds lay among the giant redwood trees or close to them. Kashaya-speaking peoples still have a detailed understanding of the redwood's botany – their conception of plants and plant communities is analogous to that used by Western botanists. Native peoples used redwood timber for house and boat construction and used other parts of the tree for medicines.

To the detriment of both forests and the native people, the powerful European culture that arrived with the settlers in the middle of the nineteenth century was based on values that were diametrically opposed to those of the indigenous peoples of the region, many of whom, along with their cultures, became extinct. The magnificent redwood trees, so pivotal to their societies, were felled in vast numbers. In 1999, however, the US government paid a lumber company $480 million in order to save the largest tract of privately owned coastal redwood forest.

THE GIANT REDWOODS

Giant redwoods and their close ancestors have been on the earth for at least 200 million years and, like their coastal cousins, once formed massive forests across the northern hemisphere. Today they are a truly relict species, occurring only in isolated groves on the western slopes of the Sierra Nevada in California.

Although the largest giant redwood in existence does not hold any records for being the oldest, tallest or broadest tree in the world, nothing can match its sheer volume. The tree known as the General Sherman, after the famous general in the American Civil War, contains an estimated 50,000 cu ft/1,415 cu m of wood. The largest trunk of any redwood is found on a tree in Alder Creek, which averages 53 ft/16 m around its base. Giant redwoods are virtually indestructible because they have fire-resistant bark. In fact, the trees need the clearing effect of forest fires to establish new seedlings successfully. They are also resistant to fungi and wood-boring insects. The main cause of death is being blown over. 'Most of the Sierra's [other] trees die of disease, fungi etc.,' wrote the Scots-born American naturalist John Muir in 1868, 'but nothing hurts the Big Tree [the giant redwood]. Barring accidents, it seems to be immortal.'

Today there are just seventy-five groves of giant redwoods left, concentrated in the King's Canyon and Sequoia National Parks, with a further three groves located in Yosemite. Where they do appear, the redwood forests seem to be healthy and reproducing well.

Giant redwood groves are found only on the slopes of upland ridges between major river canyons at 4,000–8,000 ft/1,220–2,440 m above sea-level. Here the climate is characterized by warm, dry summers and sunny winters. The latter are, however, interrupted by infrequent snowstorms, which may last from a few days to a week, leaving several feet of snow. The groves are generally tucked away from areas of high wind, but lightning strikes and thunderbolts are relatively common. Just why the giant redwoods are confined to isolated groves remains a mystery. Not a single tree is found outside these groves, even where the same climatic conditions prevail.

   The giant redwood has cinnamon-coloured bark, which may grow to a massive 18 in/45 cm thick. Unlike the slim, tapering trunk of the coast redwood, the giant's trunk

A B O V E

Young giant redwoods in Grant Grove
after the first light snow of winter.

is conical in shape and has a broad base that can reach over 40 ft/ 12 m across. Even at 200 ft/60 m above the ground, it can still be more than 20 ft/6 m in diameter. Its main branches may grow to more than 8 ft/2.4 m wide, making the tree's biggest limbs the size of large trees themselves.

The tree stands on a shallow but widely spreading root-pad, which can be enormous, radiating from the trunk for up to 300 ft/ 91 m, but seldom reaching down into the earth more than 6 ft/1.8 m. Giant redwoods reach their maximum height in the first 500 years of their life, after which lateral expansion goes on for at least 3,000 years. It is not clear when a redwood stops expanding, because there is no definite record of any giant redwood dying of old age and they continue to grow indefinitely until a natural disaster, such as a lightning strike or storm-force wind, occurs. The greatest age that has been verified from a stump by its tree rings is 3,200 years. However, John Muir claimed to have discovered a stump containing 4,000 rings.

As they age, the crowns of the trees change shape. At up to 500 years the crown is pointed like a spire, but over time it gradually becomes rounded. Fire damage can cause part of the crowns to die, as can lightning strikes.

The giant redwoods start to produce seeds after only a few years of life. Mature trees generate about 600 new cones every year and, since each cone contains several hundred healthy seeds, a tree can produce more than 100,000 seeds annually. The largest giant redwood produces some 10,000 cones and as many as two million seeds each year. The cones do not simply fall, however, and release their seeds. This function is often performed unwittingly by the chickaree, or Douglas squirrel, which finds the fleshy scales of the cones delicious. As it feeds on them, the seeds are scattered onto the forest floor. Once the seeds reach the ground, they will germinate only under exactly the right conditions.

The sugar pines and yellow pines that, along with the redwoods, form the mixed conifer forests of the Sierra Nevada, all rely on fire to create gaps in the overhead canopy and clear the forest floor. The fires also dry the redwood cones on higher branches,

THE GENERAL SHERMAN

The giant redwood tree known as the General Sherman, which stands in the Sequoia National Park of California, is the largest living thing on earth. Its vital statistics are truly impressive: weight 2.7 million lb/1.2 million kg; height 311 ft/95m; and an estimated age of 2,700 years. Its trunk at mean breast-height is 25 ft/17.6 m in diameter, while at 200 ft/60 m above the ground, it is still almost 12 ft/3.6 m across.

LEFT

For sheer volume, no living tree
today surpasses the General
Sherman. However, much larger
trees are known to have lived
in the past, which may have
been half as big again.

with the redwoods, form the mixed conifer forests of the Sierra Nevada, all rely on fire to create gaps in the overhead canopy and clear the forest floor. The fires also dry the redwood cones on higher branches, which then release their seeds onto the cooling ashes below. The action of the fires allows the seeds to fall on areas of bare mineral soil, where the sunlight is able to filter through. Where fires have been prevented, the forest floor rapidly becomes colonized by shade tolerant white firs and incense cedars, hindering redwood regeneration.

Thus the birth of the giant redwood may be likened to the rising from the ashes of the fabulous bird known as the phoenix, which eternally renews itself and has thereby become a symbol of immortality.

THE DAWN REDWOODS

The discovery of the dawn redwood (*Metasequoia glyptostroboides*) in China in 1941 made headlines across the world. Described as a 'living fossil', it was identified as one of the ancient relatives of the redwoods in California. Until 1941 it had only been known from Japanese fossil specimens dating back to between 1.5 and 6 million years ago.

The first specimen seen by an outsider stood in the remote village of Madoaoqui in the western part of Hubei province. At its base was a small shrine, to which local people brought offerings. Later a whole forest of dawn redwoods was found less than 30 miles/48 km away in the Valley of the Tiger, near Shui-se-pa.

LEFT

The distinctive red, fire-resistant bark of some of the giant redwoods on the Congress Trail in California's Sequoia National Park.

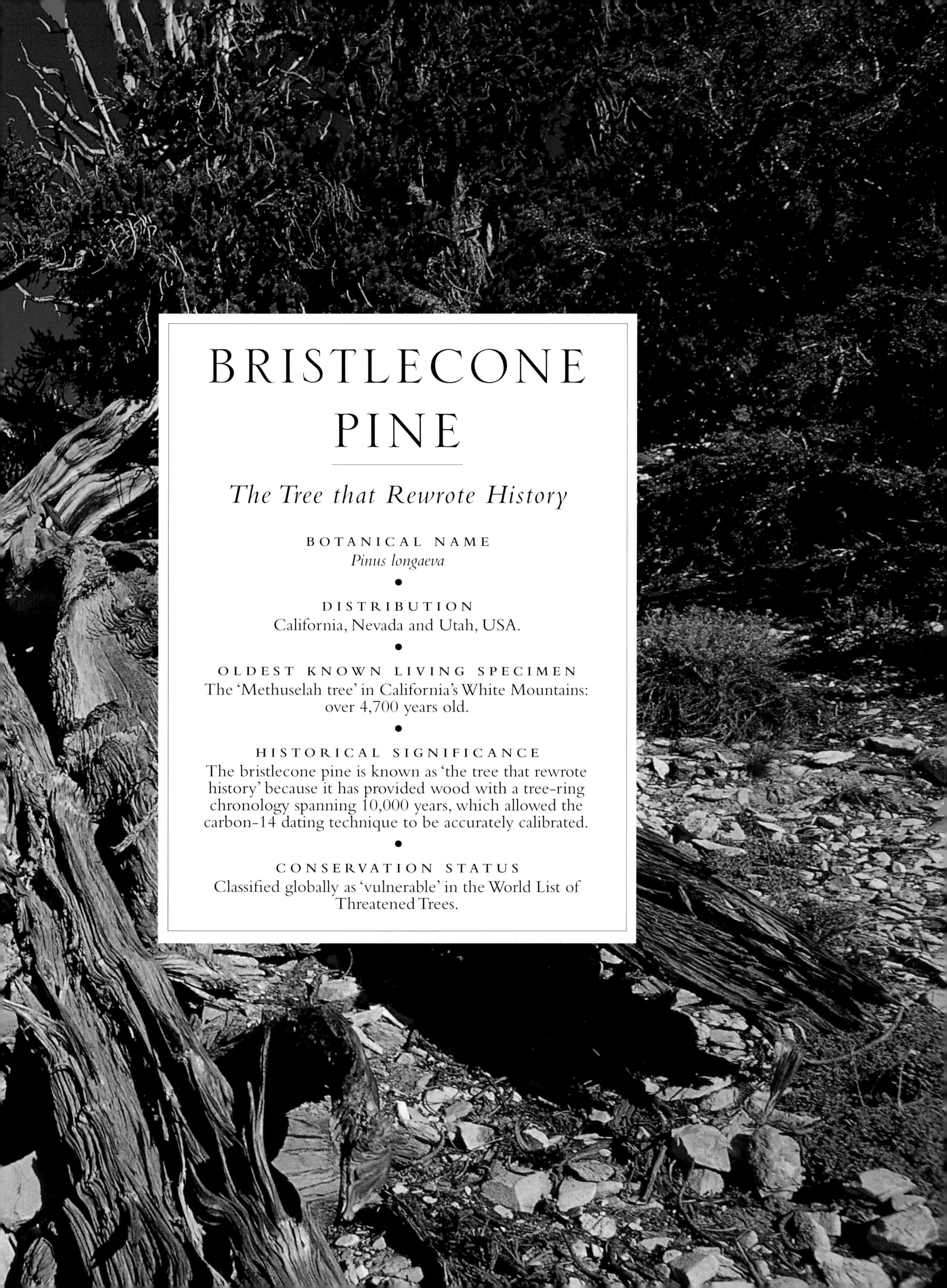

BRISTLECONE PINE

The Tree that Rewrote History

BOTANICAL NAME
Pinus longaeva

•

DISTRIBUTION
California, Nevada and Utah, USA.

•

OLDEST KNOWN LIVING SPECIMEN
The 'Methuselah tree' in California's White Mountains:
over 4,700 years old.

•

HISTORICAL SIGNIFICANCE
The bristlecone pine is known as 'the tree that rewrote
history' because it has provided wood with a tree-ring
chronology spanning 10,000 years, which allowed the
carbon-14 dating technique to be accurately calibrated.

•

CONSERVATION STATUS
Classified globally as 'vulnerable' in the World List of
Threatened Trees.

ON A BARREN MOUNTAINSIDE in eastern California's White Mountains a grove of ancient pine trees clings to life. Bleached by the sun, smoothed by the corrosive force of fierce winds bearing sand and ice, these Great Basin bristlecone pines have been moulded into grotesque natural sculptures by their inhospitable environment. Undistinguished by size or beauty, these strange trees are, however, incredibly old, and are thought to be able to reach ages in excess of 5,000 years. Here stand the Schulman Grove, and the famous Methuselah tree, which has a verifiable age of over 4,700 years, according to recent carbon-dating research. It was named by Dr Edward Schulman in 1957, after the Hebrew patriarch of the Old Testament whose long lifespan has made him a byword for longevity.

BELOW

Bristlecone pines growing on a south-facing slope in the White Mountains of California.

Looking out across an environment that has remained almost unchanged for more than 10,000 years, it seems possible to step outside time and share a moment of silence with living organisms that began their lives before the great pyramids of Egypt were constructed. Before the rise of the great empires of the Greeks, Mayans and Romans, the Methuselah tree was already one of earth's elder statesmen. It will soon begin its sixth millennium of existence.

A HOSTILE ENVIRONMENT

Two species of bristlecone pine exist. Though growing only 160 miles/260 km apart, those found on the high ridges of the Great Basin country (extending from the eastern border of California, across Nevada to Utah) reach the greatest age. The Rocky Mountain bristlecone pines (*Pinus aristata*), which reach ages of up to 1,500 years, are to be found in an area that extends from the eastern slopes of the southern Rocky Mountains in Wyoming through Colorado and down into New Mexico. The environment in which the bristlecone pines live seems an unlikely place in which to find trees of such antiquity. In fact, it is the very harshness of this environment, and the bristlecone's response to it, that has enabled this tree to achieve such great age.

The Great Basin bristlecone pines grow on steep, rocky slopes between approximately 9,000 ft/ 2,700 m and 11,500 ft/3,500 m. Between November and April each year, temperatures plummet to well below freezing and the area may receive 9 ft/2.7 m of snow. These conditions are exacerbated by the ferocious winds that scour the mountainsides. The bristlecone pine has adapted by lengthening its growing season and by putting on new growth when temperatures are much too cold for other plants.

Most of the trees are under 30 ft/9 m tall, and much of their wood – on the windward side, at least – is dead. The sparse crowns of twisted and contorted branches are supported only by narrow strips of living wood. Their ability to live in nutrient-poor soils and to conserve water has been vital to the survival of the bristlecone pines. The tree has developed special waxy leaves (needles), which may not be shed for over twenty

years, thus helping to reduce evaporation and conserve moisture; it also contains high levels of resin, which acts as a wood preservative and which is exuded to form a water-proof layer over any exposed branches. To maximize water-absorption, the tree also has an extensive network of shallow roots.

It is interesting to find that the average age of bristlecone pines on south-facing slopes in the White Mountains is typically around 1,000 years, whereas on north-facing slopes the average age rises to over 2,000 years. Entire groves of trees that are over 4,000 years old stand on the north-facing slopes, and it is amid one of these groves that the ancient Methuselah tree is found. The appearance of bristlecone forest on north- and south-facing slopes is markedly different. While the southern slopes have many healthy-looking trees, covering the hillside in quite dense forests, north-facing slopes contain trees that are much more widely spaced, squat and gnarled, with many dead branches. The severity of the environment on the north-facing slopes causes the growth rings to be more tightly packed, which in turn makes their timber more durable and the trees more long-lived. The durability of the timber is so exceptional that scientists have found dead wood, which has been shown to be 7,000 years old, lying intact close to living trees.

A forest consisting of trees that are thousands of years old can afford to regenerate at a leisurely pace. Only a handful of new seedlings needs to germinate successfully each century to ensure the forest's survival. Bristlecone pines tend not to live in isolation, but to form communities with plants such as the sage brush, mormon tea and mountain mahogany. Birds such as the mountain blue bird, the chickadee and Clark's nutcracker feed on their seeds. The last is most important for the bristlecone pine's regeneration, because it collects seeds and buries them in caches in the soil, thus helping the seedlings to gain a foothold in the inhospitable terrain.

VERIFYING THE PAST

Because bristlecone pine wood is extremely durable and can survive intact for thousands of years, scientists have been able to look not only at the ring sequences of living trees, but at those of dead trees that have remained preserved on the ground. By finding ring sequences that overlap with those from dead trees, a continuous chronology of tree rings spanning more than 10,000 years has been constructed. This has enabled valuable insights to be obtained into the climatic conditions of the past.

Such complete tree ring chronologies have also enabled the carbon-dating of artefacts to be accurately calibrated. Using wood that was aged to the exact year of its formation it was possible to test the accuracy of the carbon-14 dating method. The result was that scientists found that they had been calculating artefacts inaccurately, and many artefacts are now known to be 1,000 years older than previously thought. Bristlecone pines have hence become known as 'the trees that rewrote history'.

MONTEZUMA CYPRESS

Swamp Giant

BOTANICAL NAME
Taxodium mucronatum

•

DISTRIBUTION
Mexico (swampland or former swampland), and a few
examples in the southern United States.

•

OLDEST KNOWN LIVING SPECIMEN
The tree known as 'El Tule', growing at Santa María del
Tule, near Oaxaca, Mexico: 119 ft/36.3 m in girth, or
176 ft/53.7 m including irregularities at 3¼ ft/1 m
from the ground; estimated age: 2-4,000 years old.

•

RELIGIOUS SIGNIFICANCE
Sacred to the ancient peoples of Mexico.

•

MYTHICAL ASSOCIATIONS
Linked to Zapotec origin myths.

•

CONSERVATION STATUS
Possibly threatened.

THE MONTEZUMA CYPRESS known as El Tule is an astonishing tree. To stand before it and look up into its crown is like looking at a living Notre-Dame cathedral. Its fluted bole is reminiscent of the flying buttresses that support this architectural masterpiece. Both are immense; both demand the same degree of reverence and awe. El Tule is to be found near the village that has taken its name from the tree: Santa María del Tule, some 9 miles/14 km from the town of Oaxaca, in southern Mexico. *Tule* is not a generic name, but refers simply to this tree, which is, to use the Mexican term, an *ahuehuete* - a Montezuma or Mexican cypress (*Taxodium mucronatum*) – a species that grows almost exclusively in Mexico and has become the country's national tree. It is closely related to the swamp, southern or bald cypress (*Taxodium distichum*), which is found in the southeastern United States, and grows in a similar habitat.

Montezuma cypresses generally grow to a height of 65–100 ft/20–30 m, but may exceed 130 ft/40 m. El Tule is the largest individual in Mexico, but it is not actually the tallest; other giant trees also exist. A tree standing in Mexico City's Chapultepec Park is said to be 200 ft/60 m high, with a trunk that measures 45 ft/13 m in circumference.

The tree is an evergreen, but in the winter and spring months the foliage can appear a rusty-red colour as the new leaf buds develop. An interesting feature of these slow-growing giants is the apparent tendency of their massive, fluted and burr-covered boles to split as they grow, giving the impression, in old age, that they are not one but several trees joined together. But the distinguished Mexican botanist Maximíno Martinez, founder of Mexico's Botanical Society, who made a detailed study of the country's Montezuma cypresses, concluded in the 1950s that trees such as El Tule were not the result of a fusion of separate individuals, but of the division of the main trunk at its base.

EL TULE – THE FISSURED GIANT

In his *Historia Natural y Moral de las Indias* of 1586, the Spanish chronicler José Acosta noted, according to the local Zapotec Indians, that El Tule was a truly colossal tree some hundred years earlier, able to provide shade for 1,000 people. Though the exact date is not known, at some point during the fifteenth century it was struck by lightning, which ripped the tree asunder leaving a huge hollow, while reducing the magnificent crown to a mass of splintered branches and tattered foliage.

When the first Europeans arrived in the Mexican state of Oaxaca, where El Tule stands, it was still an impressive sight. Acosta, who provided the first written record of it, described it as a huge shell of a tree, which measured *diez y seis brazas*, or sixteen arm's lengths (a little under 89 ft/27 m) near its base, which was split into three sections. In a letter written on 7 March 1630, the Spanish priest Bernabé Cobo described the tree as follows:

'Amongst the ruins of the old village, there is a hollow tree so wide at its base, that it looks as if it would make a very capacious dwelling; it has three entrances that are so huge that you can ride through them on horseback, and there is room inside for twelve horsemen; four of us who came rode in on our horses and there was still room for another eight, I measured it outside having brought with me a ball of thread for the purpose, and it measured round its base 26 varas [57 ft/17.5 m]; … it is alive, still with many branches and leaves, although years ago a lightning strike damaged most of its branches. From here to the town of Oaxaca it is three leagues…'

Almost 400 years later the tree has risen again. The gaping hollow – estimated by contemporary researchers to have been some 129–93 sq ft/12–18 sq m in size – has been filled with new timber, and the regenerating branches have become mighty boughs that support a dome of foliage some 150 ft/46 m across, rising to a height of almost 140 ft/

During the seventeenth century the hollow inside El Tule
was reputed to have been large enough to hold twelve
men on horseback.

ABOVE AND LEFT

The Montezuma cypress is
partially deciduous, retaining
its foliage (above) until the
new year's leaves are out.
This burr (left) is known by
local people as 'El Leon'
because of its resemblance
to a lion's mane.

42 m. It is now one of the world's greatest trees and, with a bole measuring 119 ft/ 36.3 m round, or 176 ft/53.7 m including all the irregularities of the trunk, is believed to be exceeded in size only by one or two individual baobab trees in Africa. With an estimated age of 2–4,000 years, this is one of the world's most ancient trees.

ANCIENT NAME, ANCIENT ENVIRONMENT

The native Mexicans who were living in the vicinity of El Tule when the Spanish *conquistadores* arrived in the early sixteenth century were the Zapotecs. Their name for the site – later renamed Santa María by the Spanish – was *Luguiaga*, which has been roughly translated as 'amongst the reeds'. This name provides evidence to support the descriptions made by early Spanish observers of the local environment: that it was a large, reed-filled swamp, or certainly flooded for much of the time.

Before the arrival of the Spanish in Mexico the *lingua franca* in Mesoamerica was *Nahuatl* – the language of the ruling Aztecs, whose last emperor was the distinguished warrior Montezuma II (1466–1520), from whom the Montezuma cypress takes its name. *Luguiaga* was also known, more widely, by its Nahuatl name, Tollin or Tullin. This is a generic term for aquatic plants, and it evolved into the hispanicized word *Tule*. The term still used today for all Montezuma cypresses, *ahuehuete*, is also a Nahuatl word meaning, in Spanish, *viejos de agua* – literally, 'ancients of the water'.

*A*ll was darkness
when the Zapotecs were born
They burst forth from the old trees,
like the ceiba (and El Tule)
from the stomachs of the wild
beasts they were born
like the jaguar, and the lizard.

ZAPOTEC ORIGIN MYTH

It is interesting to note that El Tule and other large Montezuma cypresses are now found in locations that are distinctly arid, bearing testament to the fact that much of Mexico has become desertified over the last 2,000 years. That El Tule began its life in a swamp seems certain, but it has had to depend upon water drawn from deep down by its network of roots in order to survive. Since 1952, however, and to help compensate for the increasing scarcity of underground water, the survival of the tree has been assisted by the installation of an underground irrigation system, designed to water its roots.

In some ways El Tule is symbolic of the history of Mexico's native peoples. It was a great tree during the period in which one of the most advanced empires in the world – that of the Aztecs – was at its peak. But both the tree and the indigenous cultures of Meso-america suffered a near-fatal blow, which struck at their hearts. Gradually, over four centuries, the tree and many of the native cultures have regained their strength. Today El Tule stands proud; not just as part of Mexico's history, but as an integral part of its future.

THE LAST CELEBRATION

Swamp cypresses were revered by the ancient Mexicans and are associated with their sacred sites - it has been suggested that the church of Santa María del Tule was built on the site of an ancient Aztec place of worship. In 1586 José Acosta referred to the fact that this tree was revered, since beneath it 'people gathered to perform their ceremonial dances and superstitions'. In 1834, for the last time beneath El Tule, a ceremony was performed that was said to be a remnant of ancient Aztec ritual: it involved the sacrifice of a dove, a dance performed in honour of the tree and a special feast.

MONKEY PUZZLE

Tree of Fire and Ice

BOTANICAL NAME
Araucaria araucana

•

DISTRIBUTION
Today restricted to two small areas along the coast of
central Chile and a larger area in the Cordillera of the
Andes, on the borders of Chile and Argentina.

•

OLDEST KNOWN LIVING SPECIMEN
Approximately 2,000 years – no exact location known.

•

RELIGIOUS SIGNIFICANCE
Sacred to the Pehuenche people of south-central Chile,
who regard it as a 'mother'. They believe that
God created monkey puzzle trees for them, and that
it is their duty to protect them. Also a
'National Monument' of Chile.

•

CONSERVATION STATUS
Chilean trees are classified as 'rare' and Argentinian
as 'vulnerable' in the World List of Threatened Trees.
The Chilean monkey puzzles have also been placed on
Appendix 1 of the Convention in International Trade
in Endangered Species, meaning that all
international trade is banned.

THE MONKEY PUZZLE, with its strangely prehistoric shape, is an extraordinary tree. Many fine specimens can be seen gracing gardens and parks around the world, but the true home of the monkey puzzle is the volcanic slopes of the high Andes mountains of southern South America. Here the monkey puzzle thrives in an inhospitable terrain. Amid volcanic debris, and often clinging to precipitous slopes and the crests of hills, it seems impervious to the extremes of heat, cold and hurricane-force winds. The trees are adapted to the harshest of living conditions, including volcanic eruptions and the weight of over 3 ft/1 m of winter snow.

LIVING FOSSILS

Sometimes referred to as living fossils, monkey puzzles (*Araucaria araucana*) have an extremely ancient heritage. Remains of trees belonging to the same family have been

found, fossilized, in rocks that were formed during the Jurassic period, some 225 million years ago. About 190 million years ago the trees were one of the dominant species of the southern hemisphere, with a range that stretched from Brazil to Antarctica. Today, however, monkey puzzles are found in only a very restricted region: two small areas in the Cordillera of Nahuelbuta along the coast of central Chile, and a larger area in the Cordillera of the Andes on the borders of Chile and Argentina. Preferring north-and west-facing slopes, they grow primarily on volcanic soils, between about 2,000–6,000 ft/ 600–1,800 m above sea-level. The trees grow both in pure stands and in association with other trees, notably species of southern beech (*Nothofagus* spp.).

While young monkey puzzles resemble a pyramid or cone in shape until they begin to lose their lower branches, at about 100 years old, mature trees are distinguished by their well-defined crown, which develops some 60–100 ft/18–30 m above the ground, giving them the appearance of an open umbrella.

THE MONKEY'S PUZZLE

Monkey puzzles can live to a great age. It is common to find individuals of about 1,300 years old, while others can reach an age of 2,000 years. Growing very slowly, mature monkey puzzles develop perfectly straight, column-like trunks, which can reach nearly 165 ft/50 m in height and measure 8 ft/2.5 m at the base. The trees also develop a remarkable bark with a fascinating honeycomb pattern. In mature trees the bark can be up to 7 in/18 cm thick and may account for up to 25 per cent of the trunk's volume. It plays an important role in protecting the tree from the extremes of the Andean climate, and, importantly, is able to resist the intense heat of volcanic eruptions.

Like the bark, the curious triangular leaves of the monkey puzzle are extremely tough. They are arranged in spirals and are attached directly to the twigs and branches of the trees, and to the young trunk in early life. It is the curious arrangement of leaves and branches that was responsible for the trees' common name of 'monkey puzzler', which came into use during the late nineteenth century. Although monkeys did not live in the forests of Chile, early European observers thought that the trees would present any monkey with a challenge! According to Maud Wood-cock, writing in the 1940s, 'the monkey's puzzle consists in the monkey being able to go up the sharp points of the tree but not down them'.

While they do not support monkeys, the trees do provide the habitat for a number of rare and endangered animals. These include the puma, the Chilean pigeon and the slender-billed parakeet. One of the principal foods of the parakeet is the seeds produced by the female monkey puzzle tree. The cones that bear these seeds can grow to the size

The most remarkable thing about the trees was the bark … a perfect child's puzzle of knobbly slabs of different sizes, with five or six decided sides to each, and all fitted together with the neatness of a honey-comb.

MARIANNE NORTH

Early morning in a forest of monkey puzzle trees on the borders of Chile and Argentina. The trees thrive in the inhospitable climate, and can survive the extreme heat of summer as well as the almost intolerably harsh winter snows.

ABOVE AND LEFT

The rosette formation of spiky leaves (above) at the tip of a monkey puzzle branch. The rust-coloured male flowers (left) release pollen, which is dispersed by the wind.

of a person's head, and inside each cone may be about 200 tapering seeds, each about 1½ in/4 cm long. Though they consume many of these seeds, the parakeets also play a part in their distribution – as they force their sharp beaks inside them, the cones split, releasing the seeds, which fall onto the ground. The existence of certain dense groupings of monkey puzzle trees is said to be due to the activity of mole rats, which also inhabit the Chilean forests and bury quantities of seeds each year.

THE PEHUENCHE – PEOPLE OF THE MONKEY PUZZLES

It is the connection between monkey puzzle trees and people that is perhaps the most fascinating aspect of their existence. For one of South America's indigenous groups takes its name directly from the tree, and their lifestyle and culture are intimately related to it. These people are the Pehuenche, whose name means 'people of the monkey puzzles' – from *pehuen*, meaning 'monkey puzzle', and *che*, meaning 'people'. About 5,000 Pehuenche people currently live in the valley of the upper Bio-Bio, the longest river in the

> *The monkey puzzle is our tree. It's a symbol for us. It's a tree that God left on earth, for us, the Pehuenche. We cannot cut it down, because it gives us our daily bread. In the end, we would rather die than give up defending this tree.*
> ALFREDO MELINIR

south-central region of Chile. The Pehuenche are a traditionally resilient and independent people – part of the great Mapuche nation, the indigenous population of half the area that is today known as Argentina and Chile, whom the Incas never managed to conquer and who remained beyond the control of both the Chilean and Argentinian republics until just over a hundred years ago.

For part of each year, during late summer and early autumn, the Pehuenche live mainly as food-gatherers in the upland volcanic forests, collecting the nutritious monkey puzzle seeds. These golden brown seeds, known as piñones in Spanish, are a traditional source of food and are gathered both for immediate consumption and for storage underground, as a staple dietary item throughout the year. The harvesting of piñones is a skilful undertaking. While some seeds will be picked up from the ground, if they have fallen naturally, the Pehuenche men scale the trees with the aid of ropes, carrying long, thin poles with which to knock down more seeds. They strike the ripe cones, which

usually shatter when they are hit, sending showers of seeds falling to the ground, where the women and children quickly gather as many as they can. Large numbers of piñones are usually gathered during the harvest; a single family may be able to collect as much as 8,800 lb/4,000 kg of seeds each year, although in some years the trees produce smaller quantities of seeds.

Piñones taste something like sweet chestnuts and are generally eaten either boiled or roasted, after which the tough outer skin is removed. They are also ground into a coarse flour for making into bread and turned into a nutritious drink. Monkey puzzle seeds are fed to animals too. The Pehuenche once obtained their meat by hunting wild guanaco, a relative of the domesticated llama, but today they tend to keep small numbers of sheep and goats, and the occasional horse. During the long, harsh winters, when nearly 6½ ft/ 2 m of snow can cut off some of the remoter communities from the outside world, piñones form a useful animal-feed.

Most families also sell a proportion of the seed harvest to traders, who may travel long distances to buy direct from the Pehuenche. The piñones are then resold in lowland towns and in regional and provincial capitals, as well as the national capitals, Santiago and Buenos Aires. The Pehuenche are generally paid very little for the seeds, but the money that they generate is vital to enable them to buy many of the goods they need, including clothing and items of hardware, from nearby villages and towns.

Like so many other indigenous peoples world-wide, the Pehuenche have suffered badly from the depredations of others. Since the defeat of the Mapuche nation by Spanish armies in Chile and Argentina in 1885, their traditional lands have been continuously taken by others, and the extensive monkey puzzle forests that once supported them have been cut down by powerful timber companies. As part of this process, the Pehuenche culture has been steadily undermined, but the Pehuenche are a proud and tenacious people and it is largely due to their efforts that the monkey puzzles (certainly those in Chile) remain today.

NGUILLATUN, THE MID-SUMMER CEREMONY

A special ceremony is performed by the Pehuenche at the summer solstice (21 January) to ensure that the next piñon harvest will be plentiful. They pray, too, for an increase in their flocks of sheep and goats and for the long life of their children and elders. Wearing their traditional ponchos and special ceremonial head-dresses made of feathers, the men of the group perform a sacred dance around a young monkey puzzle tree.

LEFT

Piñon seeds are an essential part
of the Pehuenche diet; sometimes
they are even buried with the
dead to give them sustenance.

TREES WITH A SPIRIT

The monkey puzzle tree is like a mother to the Pehuenche. It is sacred, revered and respected. They may speak to it, bless it and pray to it in the course of their daily lives.

The Pehuenche regard the monkey puzzle forest as part of their extended family, or *lobpehuen*. The male tree, *domopehuen*, and the female tree, *wentrupehuen*, are believed by them to reproduce through their extensive root system. Two deities, *pehuenucha* and *pehuenkuze*, are thought to live in the forests and to influence the reproduction of the monkey puzzle trees. During their religious ceremony, *nguillatun*, a young but perfect tree is selected (perhaps only 10 ft/3 m tall) to serve as a rewe or altar, at which special prayers are said, to ensure a good harvest of seeds. This young tree is seen as a magical bridge between earth and the cosmos beyond. Some Pehuenche make a pilgrimage every year to the site of one particular, sacred monkey puzzle tree located north of the Bio-Bio river.

The Pehuenche believe that everything, including the forest, has its own spirit, or *pulli*, and that an equilibrium exists in nature that should not be upset by human beings. Although pieces of old dead wood – often found where the branches protrude from the trunk – are sometimes used as firewood, to fell a monkey puzzle would be unthinkable.

THE BATTLE TO SAVE THE TREES

Over the years, groups of Pehuenche from many different locations have tried to stop the depletion of monkey puzzle forests by timber traders. Although the monkey puzzle was declared a National Monument by the Chilean government in 1976 and felling was banned, widespread illegal felling continued none the less. Large areas of trees were also, mysteriously, set on fire, destroying many ancient forests, but still enabling timber companies to use the resilient wood for building purposes. In 1987, to make matters worse, the government gave in to pressure from the powerful timber industry and revoked the tree's protected status, leading to a free-for-all among the logging companies.

At Quinquén, near the small town of Lonquimay, the Meliñir family of Pehuenche decided that they had had enough. Enlisting the support of CODEFF, Chile's leading environmental group, their efforts prompted the launching of a nationwide campaign to protect the remaining forest. After a bitterly fought campaign, the government declared the area in question a national reserve, limiting the local people's access to their monkey puzzle trees. As Ricardo Meliñir, the *lonqo* or spiritual leader, put it, 'After all these years defending the trees, it's a scandal. We want people everywhere to know what has happened here.' Unfortunately, the situation remains unresolved.

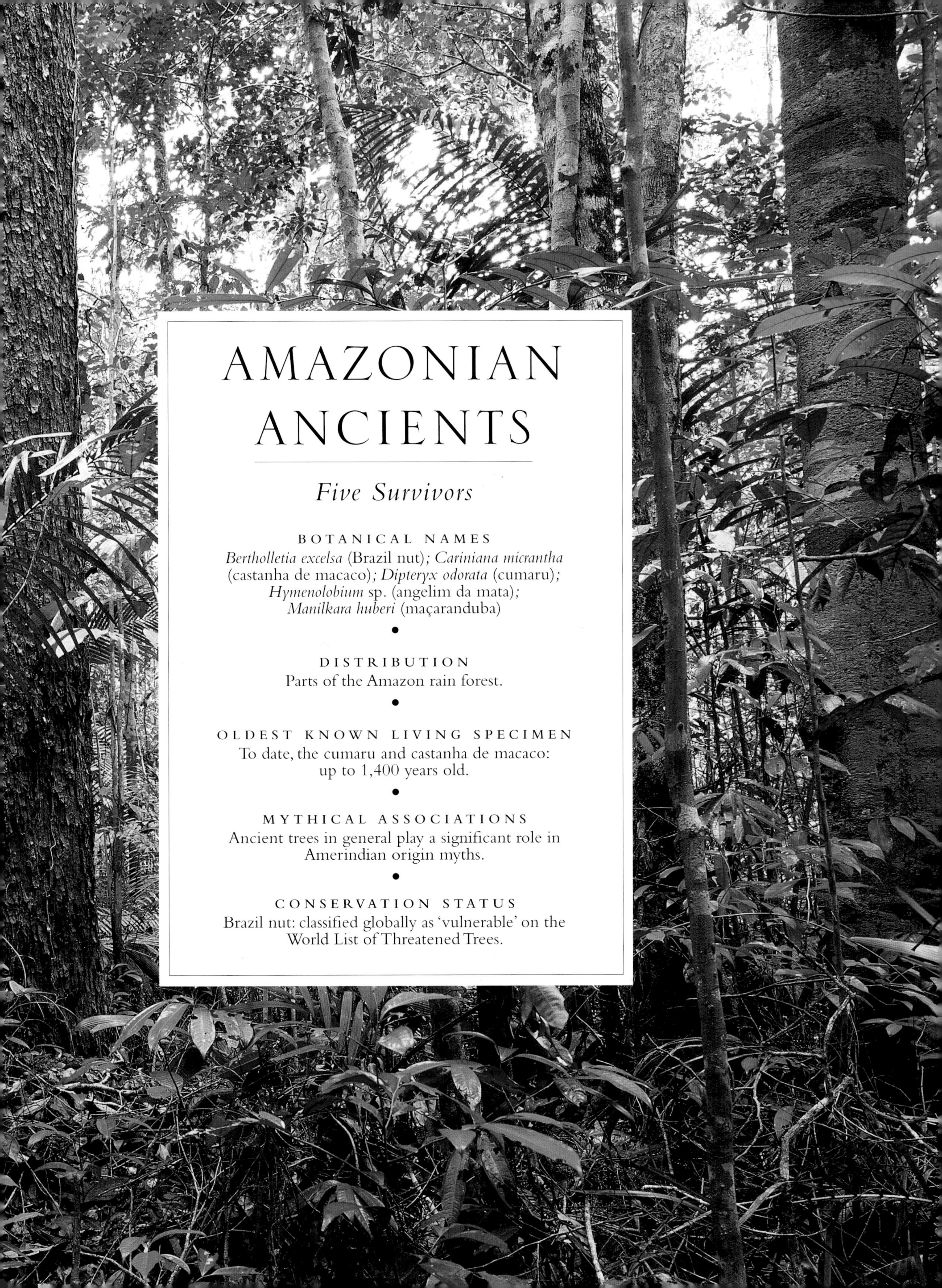

AMAZONIAN ANCIENTS

Five Survivors

BOTANICAL NAMES
Bertholletia excelsa (Brazil nut); *Cariniana micrantha*
(castanha de macaco); *Dipteryx odorata* (cumaru);
Hymenolobium sp. (angelim da mata);
Manilkara huberi (maçaranduba)

•

DISTRIBUTION
Parts of the Amazon rain forest.

•

OLDEST KNOWN LIVING SPECIMEN
To date, the cumaru and castanha de macaco:
up to 1,400 years old.

•

MYTHICAL ASSOCIATIONS
Ancient trees in general play a significant role in
Amerindian origin myths.

•

CONSERVATION STATUS
Brazil nut: classified globally as 'vulnerable' on the
World List of Threatened Trees.

FOR MANY CENTURIES THE GREAT Amazon rain forest of Brazil has inspired awe and respect in all who have experienced its wonders at first hand. Charles Darwin (1809–82) wrote: 'Delight … is a weak term to express the feelings of a naturalist who, for the first time, has wandered by himself in a Brazilian forest … the beauty of the flowers, the glossy green of the foliage, but, above all, the general luxuriance of the vegetation filled me with admiration.'

The pioneering studies of naturalists and explorers, such as Alexander von Humboldt (1769–1859), Alfred Wallace (1823–1913) and Henry Walter Bates (1825–92) helped to reveal Amazonia's fantastic natural wealth. Yet today, despite all the research that has taken place, the Amazon continues to be an awesome and mysterious place that holds many secrets. The luxuriant forest, often shrouded in gently swirling mists, still conceals Indian peoples who have yet to make contact with the modern world; countless species of plant and insect that are unknown to science; and, until very recently, it also kept hidden the fact that many of its great trees may be over 1,000 years old.

CATASTROPHES AND MYTHS

We now know that some of Amazonia's grand old trees have survived periods of environmental disruption, such as droughts and possibly widespread fires, which are linked to climatic disturbances caused by El Niño, the warming of the eastern tropical Pacific. Climatological research has shown that devastating El Niño events occurred in the Amazon 1,500, 1,000, 700 and 450 years ago. Interestingly, many Amerindian myths exist about the 'creator' causing great winds, devastating fires and floods, which may be linked to the influence of El Niño. One myth of the Urubu people of northern Brazil recounts how the creator 'Mair' set fire to the world and then put the flames out with a flood of water. After he had done this a number of times the Indians complained to him, saying that 'each time they had to climb trees

and might be turned into sloths, if they screwed their eyes up against the smoke, or into frogs, if they slid down the tree for a drink before the flood had gone'.

The traditional importance of large and ancient trees to Amazonian Indians cannot be underestimated. Most indigenous groups have had not only an intimate knowledge of the variety of species that exist locally but also an understanding of the ages of particular ancient trees. It is a recurring theme in South and Central American Indian mythology that a large or ancient tree is present in the origin myth. The creator, or the first people, often emerge from such trees, and most of the myths indicate exactly which tree was involved. In myths of the Urubu, for instance, the creator emerges from a jatoba tree, the vulture emerges from the pau d'arco, while people come from the 'wira pitang or red-wood tree'.

I could only wonder at the sombre shades, scarce illuminated by a single direct ray of the sun, the enormous size and height of the trees, most of which rise in huge columns a hundred feet [30 m] or more without throwing out a single branch; the furrowed stems of others; the extraordinary creepers which wind around them, hanging in long festoons from branch to branch, sometimes curling and twisting on the ground like great serpents, then sprouting to the very tops of the trees, thence throwing lower roots and fibres which hang waving in the air, or twisting round each other to form ropes and cables of every variety and size.

ALFRED WALLACE, 1889

THE DISCOVERY OF AMAZONIA'S ANCIENTS

For many years it was considered unlikely that any Amazonian tree could live to great age because of the accelerated rates of growth and decay that occur in the rain forest. However, research carried out during the late 1990s, in the forest near the Amazonian city of Manaus, is set to revolutionize our understanding not just of ancient Amazonian trees, but also of the timescale of the ecological cycles of which they are a part.

In the past it was difficult to assess the true age of Amazonian trees because they do not exhibit the characteristic tree rings that most species native to temperate forests display. Tree rings are formed as a result of the growth put on during a distinct growing

The straight-trunked cumaru is readily identifiable by its distinctive pale bark.

ABOVE AND RIGHT

Latex from the maçaranduba (above) is still used to make chewing gum, although the tree has been widely felled for its timber. Brazil-nut pods (right), which may weigh as much as 3⅓ lb / 1.5 kg, usually contain between ten and twenty-five nuts.

season. As the seasons in Amazonia are less clearly defined than those in temperate regions, in many species annual rings are irregular or do not exist at all. In the case of the Amazonian trees, however, radiocarbon-dating was employed. From their studies of the tree stumps left behind by a large logging operation near Manaus, Niro Higuchi (at the Instituto Nacional de Pesquisas in Manaus), Jeffrey Chambers and Joshua Schimel (of the Department of Ecology at the University of California, Santa Barbara) have shown that four species of Amazonian trees definitely live to over 1,000 years of age: the castanha de macaco, the cumaru, the angelim da mata and the maçaranduba. Twenty trees from thirteen different species were studied and their ages were established to range between 200 and 1,400 years, the oldest being castanha de macaco and cumaru trees.

All four species are tall, elegant trees, which produce a dome of lush foliage, emerging from the canopy at some 100–165 ft/30–50 m from the ground. But they are not giants, like the colossal kauris of New Zealand or the redwoods of North America. Their reasonably slender trunks, which measure only 3¼–13 ft/1–4 m in diameter, gave no particular reason to believe that they were especially old. However, the trunks of all four trees are supported by buttresses to varying degrees.

Of the fifteen Cariniana species native to South America, the castanha de macaco or 'monkey nut' (*Cariniana micrantha*), which is related to the Brazil nut, produces – as its name suggests – fruits that are relished in particular by monkeys. The castanha de macaco is a tall, emergent tree whose foliage is visible as a pale-green dome rising above the surrounding canopy. With its distinctive mottled grey and salmon-coloured bark, the elegant cumaru (*Dipteryx odorata*) is, like the castanha de macaco, a prized timber tree. It is also the source of tonka beans. Developing from the tree's eye-catching purple flowers, and with a distinctive odour of new-mown hay, these beans were once widely used in Europe as a tonic and aromatic, because of the compound coumarin that they contain. They are still used for flavouring and perfumery today

The maçaranduba (*Manilkara huberi*), which can reach 131 ft/ 40 m or more in height, is interesting in a different way. It is one of a number of trees that has continued to intrigue many visitors to Amazonia – at least since the time of explorers such as Alexander von Humboldt and Richard Spruce (1817–93) – who noticed that the white, sweetish-tasting latex that oozed from the bark when cut could be drunk like milk, without any harmful effects.

The angelim da mata is one of ten *Hymenolobium* species. It is distinguished by its beautiful, flaking bark – a deep red in colour – and by its pink or magenta flowers. The name of the tree is believed to refer to the delicate, papery surround to its seeds, which enable them to float to the ground like 'little angels of the forest'.

The best known of Amazonia's ancient trees, however, is the Brazil nut (*Bertholletia excelsa*), which occurs across a wide area of the Amazon. A magnificent tree, its distinctive silhouette can be seen rising to heights of over 164 ft/50 m in the rain forest. Many groves of mature Brazil-nut trees in the Amazon today were planted long ago by Amazonian Indians.

When Chambers, Schimel and Higuchi carried out their pioneering research, the Brazil nut was at that time the only tree in Amazonia to have been carbon-dated. The one individual concerned was only 7¼ ft/2.25 m in diameter, but was found to be 500 years old. It now looks likely that far more ancient Brazil-nut trees exist.

Who knows how many other tree species that live to 1,000 years the Amazon may contain?

*P*erhaps no country in the world contains such an amount of vegetable matter on its surface as the valley of the Amazon. Its entire extent, with the exception of some very small portions, is covered with one dense and lofty primeval forest, the most extensive and unbroken which exists upon the earth.

ALFRED WALLACE , 'VEGETATION OF THE AMAZON VALLEY'

BELOW

The striking red bark of an ancient angelim da mata tree stands out against its green surroundings.

YEW

The Guardian of Time

BOTANICAL NAME
Taxus baccata

•

DISTRIBUTION
Europe, North Africa and West Asia.

•

OLDEST KNOWN LIVING SPECIMEN
The Fortingall yew, Perthshire, Scotland: at least 5,000
years old, possibly 9,000 years old.

•

RELIGIOUS SIGNIFICANCE
Sacred to early Indo-European peoples, such as
Celtic and Nordic tribes.

•

MYTHICAL ASSOCIATIONS
Believed by ancient peoples to be immortal
and a symbol of everlasting life.

THERE IS SOMETHING AWE-INSPIRING and magical about an ancient yew. With its massive trunk and evergreen crown it must have appeared immortal to our ancestors, standing as a silent witness to the passage of time. In the deepest winter months, it was not only green but often ablaze with flame-red berries and filled with the excited chatter of birds – an island of life in a barren landscape.

Many of Europe's most ancient yew trees began their lives before recorded history, before the Egyptians built the pyramids, and while mammoths were still roaming the earth. With the development of carbon-dating techniques, palaeontologists have been able to date fossils with increasing accuracy, and fossil remains of a yew species that is virtually indistinguishable from the modern tree have now been dated to almost one million years old. The discovery of yew trees preserved in some of Europe's peat bogs has shown that they were more numerous and widespread before the last Ice Age, which ended 1.7 million years ago. The trees seem to have a presence, an aura, acting as they do as a living link with history. Perhaps no other tree is so deeply interwoven with the ancient history of Indo-European people, or holds the same fascination and sense of mystery.

ABOVE

The yew tree differs from true conifers because it produces a single seed surrounded by a fleshy covering.

OPPOSITE

Yews are a familiar sight in graveyards, where Christian churches were built on ancient pagan burial grounds.

THE IMMORTAL TREE

The common yew (*Taxus baccata*) can be found growing wild in most of Europe, extending from Scandinavia and Estonia in the north as far south as the mountains of North Africa, and from Ireland in the west to the western Himalayas in the east, where it will grow at up to 11,000 ft/3,350 m. Common yews form woodlands with a closed canopy, especially on steep valley sides, although few such woodlands now remain in the modern landscape. However, yew woods appear to thrive better than many other trees on steep chalk slopes, and what is acknowledged as the finest yew forest in Europe is found on the chalk downland of Kingley Vale in Sussex, England.

Common yews are not famous for the great heights they reach, but for the enormously thick trunks that they form in old age. With their deep reddish- or purplish-brown bark, and trunks that are often deeply fissured and fluted, they can measure up to

BELOW

*The dark shade cast by yews in the wood
of Kingley Vale in Sussex prevents any other
plants growing beneath them.*

THE YEW LONGBOW

There is evidence to suggest that yew weapons have been important to
the people of Europe for tens of thousands of years. The oldest wooden
artefact ever discovered is a yew spear unearthed at Clacton in England,
which was in use more than 250,000 years ago. Both Homer and Virgil
in ancient Greece noted that the best bows were made of yew wood. The
longbow was the principal weapon for about five hundred years from the
time of the Norman Conquest in 1066.

LEFT

*Yew is ideal for bows because there is
a clearly visible difference in colour
between the heartwood and the
sapwood. The bows need to be cut so
that sapwood is on the inside of the
curve and the highly elastic
heartwood, which has great tensile
strength, is on the outside.*

56 ft/17 m in girth, becoming hollow in extreme old age. Another distinctive feature is their majestic spreading crown – often conical in shape – of intensely dark green foliage.

Mature yew trees grow extremely slowly. The conventional method of dating trees is from their growth rings, and yews of over 20 ft/6 m in girth, with 80–100 rings per inch/2.5 cm in the outer 6 in/15 cm, could be well over 1,000 years old. However, this method alone is not enough to enable us to date living yews accurately, as it is almost impossible to find any one piece of wood as old as the whole tree. Most ancient yews become hollow over time, which means that conventional dating methods are not easy to apply. To make matters more complicated, growth in the tree can be very uneven. Some yews apparently lie dormant for a very long time while others, such as the Crowhurst yew, may grow by only infinitesimally small amounts over extended periods.

The dating of ancient yews has had to rely on other methods: the extrapolation of growth curves, from careful studies of trees whose planting dates are known, and measurements taken from pieces of ancient wood. Such measurements have indicated that yews over 30 ft/9 m in girth could have been growing at the time of Christ. The yew at Fortingall in Scotland, whose trunk has now split, was measured in the late eighteenth century at about 52 ft/16 m in girth and may be up to 9,000 years old. There are several other yews that are more than 5,000 years old, and possibly over 100 trees that are in excess of 1,000 years.

Yew wood is one of the strongest and most durable woods known. However, having reached extreme old age (i.e. 2,000 years or so) the tree's root system slowly pulls the tree apart, causing fissures to appear or deepen. As this happens, the heartwood of the yew is exposed to the elements and usually rots away, leaving a huge hollow. Such hollows can be as much as 10 ft/3 m across. Over the centuries some hollows have been put to ingenious uses – in the nineteenth century, the Crowhurst yew, for example, was fitted out as a room with tables and chairs, and on one side a doorway was cut.

Although the tree becomes hollow, the yew's life is by no means at an end. It has been suggested that this characteristic may be part of the yew tree's strategy for survival, in that it becomes better able to resist strong winds by allowing them to pass through it. In time, new wood will begin to grow over and encase the old shell, producing layers of different textures and colours, with enormous tensile strength. The hollowing of the tree also enables the yew to renew itself, over many hundreds of years, from the inside out. A branch may grow down from the tree, embedding itself in the soil in the middle of the hollow trunk, thus forming an aerial root. In time this will become a new tree.

LEFT

The trunk of the Crowhurst yew in Surrey is estimated
to be more than 4,000 years old.

More common than this, though, is for a branch or branches to dip down and slowly grow towards the ground outside the tree. Eventually new trees will grow up around the central one, forming a circular grove. Left undisturbed, this process can continue indefinitely, so that further groves are formed. Sadly, no fully established examples of yew groves exist today. Most of the trees old enough to re-establish themselves in this way are situated in churchyards, where it has often been deemed necessary to cut off branches growing near the ground.

Much of what we know about the extraordinary longevity of the yew is due to the tireless research and personal conviction of one man – Allen Meredith. First made aware of the importance of the yew in dreams during the 1970s, Meredith has since researched all aspects of the tree's history, tracing historical references and taking measurements of ancient British yews. Through his work he has convinced botanists that many yews are thousands of years old, refuting the established belief that the maximum age a yew could reach was 800 years. The astonishing longevity that yew trees are now known to achieve and their extraordinary ability to renew themselves from a state of great decay have set them apart from most other European trees and given rise to the concept of their immortality. As the distinguished late dendrologist Alan Mitchell said, 'We've now more or less agreed that these trees can be more than 4,000 years old. In fact, there appears to be no theoretical end to this tree, no reason for it to die.'

THE TREE OF LIFE

The yew's extraordinary ability to renew itself from decay must have been awe-inspiring to our ancestors, and it is not hard to imagine how it could have found symbolic expression as the Tree of Life. The Old Testament contains references to a tradition of tree worship, and in Mesopotamia the Tree of Life was a dominant deity for Middle Eastern civilizations from as early as 5000 BC. The Egyptian goddess, Isis, was also linked with a Tree of Life, which may have been a yew.

The massive yew at Tandridge in Surrey displays the natural tendency for the branches to dip down and form new trees where they touch the ground.

THE YEW CULT

No one knows who first venerated the yew, but it appears to have been central to the ancient animistic religions of Europe and western Asia, which revered the fertility of nature and which honoured and celebrated its renewal each year. To adherents of these religions, evergreen trees were associated with immortality. The ancient celebration that marks the winter solstice is a festival that appears to have been held since the dawn of human history. Meredith believes that a European yew cult, involving the worship of the tree's scarlet fruits and its evergreen leaves, was 'one of the first expressions of

The snake-like, exposed roots of an old yew in the grounds of Waverley Abbey in Surrey.

There is a Yew-tree, pride of Lorton Vale,
Which to this day stands single in the midst
Of its own darkness, as it stood of yore:
Not loth to furnish weapons for the bands
Of Umfraville or Percy ere they marched
To Scotland's heaths; or those that crossed the sea
And drew their sounding bows at Azincourt,
Perhaps at earlier Crécy, or Poitiers.
Of vast circumference and gloom profound
This solitary Tree! a living thing
Produced too slowly ever to decay;
Of form and aspect too magnificent
To be destroyed.

WILLIAM WORDSWORTH (1770–1850), 'THE PRIDE OF LORTON VALE'

religious awe' and that it was from these ancient mid-winter celebrations that the sophisticated beliefs represented by the Norse myths developed. The tree played a central part in the Nordic beliefs that held sway in the northern forests of Europe and which were marked by the worship of gods such as Odin and Ullr, the Norse god of archers, who was strongly connected to the yew. These in turn gave rise to belief in concepts such as Yggdrasil, the Tree of Life. Later peoples, too, are known to have held strong beliefs associated with the yew – the Romans believed that it gave the souls of the dead safe passage to the after-life, while the Saxons planted thousands of yew trees in Britain to mark the interment of their dead.

Although it is difficult to determine the actual development of an Indo-European yew cult, it is likely that both people and religious ideas spread west across Europe, eventually reaching Britain in 4000 BC. The Celts, who reached their maximum range in the third century AD, stretching from Turkey to Spain and Ireland, are often associated with veneration of the oak, but yew trees were certainly sacred to them and were planted on their holy sites. Many Celtic tribes are known to have taken their name from the yew, such as the Iverni of southern Ireland. The etymology of the word 'yew' is fascinating: despite its many spellings in a range of ancient and modern languages across Europe, the sound remains virtually the same – *yr* in old Norse, *yewar* in Celtic, *iva* in Middle Latin and *iubhar* in Gaelic.

ANCIENT YEWS, OLD CHURCHES

To the Christian Church, the ancient fertility cults that centred on the yew were blasphemous and to be abhorred. However, instead of destroying the ancient sacred sites and 'pagan' practices that had flourished for so long, the policy of the Church was to Christianize them. It is significant that what was to become the holy island of Iona and the centre of early Christianity in Britain was previously the centre of a yew cult. Indeed, the name Iona was translated as 'Island of the Yews'.

Churches were built on 'pagan' sites and Allen Meredith has discovered that the positioning of the church in relation to the yew or yews in the churchyard can indicate the antiquity of the trees themselves. A siting to the north of the church suggests a tree dating back to Neolithic times (*c.* 4000–2000 BC). The yew trees that appear to be the oldest in Britain – all over 5,000 years old – are situated in this northerly position. Those found to the east and west of the church date back to Celtic times, while those to the south or southwest tend to indicate Saxon sites. The Christian Church also used parts of the trees themselves as important symbols. Yew branches were blessed and some were

A B O V E
——
*One of the ancient yews in
Borrowdale, Cumbria, that inspired
William Wordsworth's poem
'The Fraternal Four'.*

burnt, so that their ashes could be used on Ash Wednesday. For centuries, yew branches were used as a substitute for the 'palm fronds' displayed on Palm Sunday.

The yew was considered a powerful guardian against the forces of evil. Remnants of a belief in the once-powerful magic of the yew tree have survived in talismans made of yew and in the fact that, throughout Europe, yews were often planted near homesteads in order to bring protection, although it was said to be unlucky to bring a yew's branches inside. To cut down a yew tree in a churchyard, or to burn or damage the branches, is also said to be very unlucky.

Yew expert Allen Meredith considers that the destruction of ancient yews will bring far more than just bad luck upon us. He calls the yew 'the watcher, the guardian of the planet', and feels that our very survival is linked to the continued survival of these magnificent trees.

OAK

Spirit of the Wildwood

BOTANICAL NAME
Quercus robur (the common, English or pendunculate oak)

•

DISTRIBUTION
Across Europe, from Ireland in the west to Asia
Minor in the east, and south to the Mediterranean
coast of western North Africa.

•

OLDEST KNOWN LIVING SPECIMEN
Widest bole: possibly the Bowthorpe oak in
Lincolnshire, England: 41¾ ft/12.7 m in girth; oldest:
possibly the Kongeegen or Royal oak, in Nordskoven,
Denmark, or the Chêne de mon travail, in the
Charente region of France, both said to
be around 2,000 years old.

•

RELIGIOUS SIGNIFICANCE
Sacred to the ancient Norse, Germanic and Celtic
peoples, and to the Greeks and Romans; some
individual trees have become shrines.

•

MYTHICAL ASSOCIATIONS
Associated with the gods of thunder and lightning
among ancient European peoples, and with fertility;
individual trees have also become associated with
figures of legend, such as Robin Hood.

BELOW

The Major oak in Sherwood Forest is said locally to have been the tree beneath which Robin Hood met his merry men.

O F ALL THE NATIVE TREES OF EUROPE, the mighty oak has held a special fascination since the earliest times. With its distinctive broad crown, supported by a massive trunk in old age, this handsome tree has become an enduring symbol of strength, protection, durability, courage and truth.

Vast forests dominated by oaks – the common oak (*Quercus robur*) and the sessile oak (*Quercus petraea*) – once stretched unbroken across huge areas of western Europe, shaping the lives of prehistoric peoples. To Norse and Germanic peoples and to the Celts, the oak was a sacred tree, and it was among holy oak groves that they made contact with their powerful gods.

A connection between the oak and ancient European storm gods developed long ago. Oaks are in fact more likely to be struck by lightning than most other European woodland trees because of their size and because their electrical resistance is low. Belief in such a connection appears to have been common to the Aryan peoples who came to inhabit much of Europe and parts of Asia before the birth of Christ. To these people, the mighty oak formed a channel through which the power of the sky gods could reach the mortals on earth – visibly demonstrated when a tree was struck by lightning and caught fire.

The kindling of fire from an oak log on midsummer's eve was a Celtic practice, associated with fertility and probably accompanied by human sacrifice. Oak was also traditionally used for the Yule log that was burnt at the winter solstice, in the hope of drawing back the sun to warm the earth. (In Rome, the Vestal Virgins – priestesses of Vesta, the Roman goddess of the hearth – also used oak wood for their perpetual fires.)

The oak tree occupied a central position in the religious practices of the Celtic priests, the Druids. The

LEFT

Oaks have a much higher chance of being hit by lightning than other trees, and this led in the past to their association with European gods of thunder.

name Druid means 'oak man' and is said to derive from the Greek word for oak, *druz*. The Druids revered the tree, as they believed it embodied the strength, power and energy of their mighty god Esus, and ritual sacrifices in his honour were performed amid their sacred groves. Mistletoe, the semi-parasitic shrub which can cling to the oak's branches under the right conditions, was also regarded as sacred, since it was thought to be a guardian of the tree.

Germanic tribes dedicated the oak to Donar, while in Norse mythology, the oak was sacred to Thor, who drove his chariot across the heavens and controlled the weather. Both were gods of thunder, and if a tree was struck by lightning, pieces of the splintered wood were kept as protective charms. At the end of the first century AD the Roman historian Cornelius Tacitus (*c.* 55–120) mentions oak groves in northwest Europe that were especially sacred to Thor, many of which were subsequently destroyed by Christian missionaries. Belief in this deity was so strong that 'Thor's day' – now Thursday – was dedicated to him right across the Germanic world and regarded as a holy day.

The oak was likewise revered by the ancient Greeks and Romans. The tree became sacred to the Greek god Zeus, the supreme being associated with the sky and weather, and to the principal Roman god Jupiter – the oak's association with lightning strikes, which were the special weapons of both these deities, was particularly significant.

To the ancients, the oak tree's special presence and powers included those of an oracle. In Homer's *Iliad*, Odysseus travelled to the famous oak that grew at Dodona to find out from its 'lofty foliage' the plans of Zeus. And according to the Greek poet Hesiod's *Catalogues*, the priestesses, who took the form of doves and lived in the tree's hollow trunk, imparted 'all kinds of prophecy' to those who travelled there.

ANCIENT OAK MYSTERY

The theory that the oak was a special tree to our ancestors, connected with the supernatural, was strengthened in Britain in 1998. On the north Norfolk coast an extraordinary, mysterious structure was revealed by the shifting sands: an enormous oak tree stuck into the ground, with the stumps of its roots pointing upwards, surrounded by an oval ring of no fewer than fifty-four oak trunks. This unique find, which may be the remains of an early Bronze Age tree temple, has been carbon-dated at 4,000 years old, making it as old as Stonehenge.

L E F T

Archaeologist Mark Brennand has suggested that the purpose of the temple was 'excarnation'. The central upturned oak forms a kind of altar, a platform on which the bodies of the dead might be exposed.

TREE OF STRENGTH

When the Swedish botanist Carolus Linnaeus (1707–78) used the term *robur* (from the Latin word for 'strength') to describe the common oak (*Quercus robur*), he was referring to two features that set it apart from many other trees: the robustness of the living tree and the great strength of its timber. The oak is particularly rugged and hardy and is able to withstand attacks by pests and diseases, as well as exposure to extremes of temperature and drought.

Even during the longest and most severe droughts, oaks seem to show no signs of suffering. This is true both of those that commonly grow in clay soils, which hold water well, and those found in drier, sandy regions. The vast edifice of trunk and crown is anchored to the ground by a network of tenacious roots. For the first few years of its life the oak sends a large tap root into the soil, but other lateral roots soon develop, which stabilize the tree as well as drawing up water (around 20 gallons/90 litres a day).

Oak timber is synonymous with strength and durability. For thousands of years it has been used for construction purposes wherever permanence is required. Tree-ring evidence has proved that oak wood was being used in Germany some 9,000 years ago and in Ireland 7,200 years ago. In Scandinavia archaeologists have found that coffins were hollowed out of oak trunks from the early Bronze Age, in order to give safe passage to the dead during their long journey to the next world. In Britain, King Arthur's Round Table was reputedly made from an enormous piece of oak, and the oak coffin (made from a hollowed-out tree) that rests in Somerset's Glastonbury Abbey is said to contain his remains. Oak bark was also used extensively for tanning leather, and oak charcoal for iron furnaces. By the time of Elizabeth I (1533–1603), so many oaks had been felled that laws were passed to protect them for future use, and extensive planting was subsequently carried out in the Royal Forests.

BELOW

The oak tree's foliage provides food for a greater number of different insects than other trees, supporting some 500 species.

SURVIVORS FROM THE WILDWOOD

Today, only tiny remnants of the extensive forests that clothed much of northern Europe 7,000 years ago, and in which oaks predominated, remain. Sometimes known as the 'wildwood', these forests have been steadily cleared since Neolithic times. During the reign of Henry VIII (1491–1547) one-third of England was still clothed with oak woods; today only about 494,220 acres/200,000 hectares of England's ancient woodland are still covered by native trees and shrubs. Britain, and in particular England and Wales, have the biggest and best array of ancient trees in northwest Europe, many of which are oaks: this is largely the accidental result of Britain's history of land-use, especially its ancient systems of forest management. Oaks were also commonly planted as boundary markers between shires and parishes, or left as hedgerow trees. The oak is, therefore, still widely regarded as the 'father of trees' – a tangible link with the wildwood of long ago. It has become an unofficial emblem of England and been adopted as the national tree of the Irish Republic.

Many of the oaks that are outstanding today (because of their vast proportions and great age) now grow alone, as isolated individuals, often in parkland or fields, and sometimes in more urban settings. Their continued existence is fiercely defended by tree-lovers and by those who view the oak as a magical protector of a rural way of life that many would like to retrieve.

An astonishing number of oak-tree species exist: over 600 in all, native to northern temperate regions. In spite of its name, the English or common oak is found right across Europe to Asia Minor and the Caucasus mountains, and south to the Mediterranean coast of western North Africa. Although very similar in its general appearance to the sessile or durmast oak, which has a similar range, it is the common oak that has produced most of the gnarled and ancient oaks.

As when, upon a trancèd summer-night,
Those green-robed senators of mighty woods,
Tall oaks, branch-charmèd by the earnest stars,
Dream, and so dream all night without a stir.

JOHN KEATS (1795-1821), 'HYPERION'

There is still some debate about just how old the most ancient oaks of Europe really are. The noted British dendrologist and co-founder of the Tree Register of the British Isles, Alan Mitchell (1922–95), felt that claims to the great age of oaks were often misguided. By plotting girth against age, he showed that in their early years oaks actually grow quite fast, on average, about 1 in/2.5 cm per year, and that maturity is reached by about 250 years, after which time the tree will slowly begin to die. 'The only open question', he wrote, 'is how much and for how long an oak over 25 ft [7.6 m] round can decrease in vigour, and so how much older than, say, 250 years it can be … to be 1,000 years old, it should be around 40 ft [12 m] round.'

The dating technique refined by dendrologist John White disagrees with the assumption that the trunk of the oak (and other ancient trees) will grow fairly constantly at about 1 in/2.5 cm per annum, and shows many ancient trees to be twice as old as previously thought. White's method is based on measurements of the tree's girth, and comparison of this data with other trees of the same species, size and, wherever possible, known planting dates on comparable sites. It also recognizes that trees grow at different rates during different phases of their lives: formative, middle and old age.

It is generally agreed, however, that the biggest and oldest oaks tend to be pollards. From medieval times until about 1800 pollarding was standard practice in many

woodlands: it involved cutting off the trunk about 8 ft/2.4 m up, when the tree was about
twenty years old and at intervals thereafter, so that successive crops of smallwood or round-
wood (wood of a smaller diameter than the trunk, and useful for a variety of purposes)
could be harvested later. The tree would resprout rapidly, and within a few years would
put on a much greater volume of foliage – often on about six upraised branches – than
would a 'maiden', or uncut, tree. While a maiden tree depends on its original trunk, and
dies when this does, a pollarded tree can continue to put out new shoots into old age,

*An ancient oak, like this tree in Dorset,
still creates an impressive silhouette when
hundreds of years old. The oak has
always been synonymous with
strength and durability.*

long after the original trunk has become hollow, is more vigorous in its growth and its bole grows faster in diameter. For these reasons, pollards are generally the oldest oaks and those with the biggest trunks.

The tree currently considered to have the greatest girth anywhere in the British Isles (and possibly in Europe), measuring 41¾ ft/12.7 m in girth, is at Bowthorpe, near Bourne, on the flat Lincolnshire fens. With a hollow inside that measures 9 ft/2.7 m by 6 ft/1.8 m, it has been described by tree enthusiast Thomas Pakenham as 'a cave with branches growing from the roof'. It was apparently hollow nearly 200 years ago, when it was described as having 'ever since the memory of older inhabitants or their ancestors been in the same state of decay. The inside of the body is hollow and the upper is used as a pigeon-house'. A floor was installed in 1768 and benches added around the inside, so that the Squire of Bowthorpe Park could dine inside with twenty guests. It is generally agreed that this tree is probably about 1,000 years old.

Another close contender, in terms of size, is the tall and beautiful tree that stands in Fredville Park in Kent. Known as the Majesty oak, it is almost 40 ft/12.2 m in girth. Thomas Pakenham has described it as adding 'to the grace of monarch the scale of a mammoth'. With a main trunk that is hollow from top to bottom – a length of about 30 ft/9 m – it is not clear whether this is a pollard or a maiden tree, but it is estimated to be not more than 600 years old.

In Moccas Park in Herefordshire, the ancient pollarded oaks, fondly called the 'crusty old men of Moccas', were described in 1876 by the clergyman and diarist Francis Kilvert (1840–79) as: 'grey, gnarled low-browed, knock-kneed, bowed, bent, huge, strange, long-armed, deformed, hunch-backed, misshapen oak men.' John White believes that these trees are also over 1,000 years old.

Other ancient oaks in Britain include the Marton oak in Cheshire, still flourishing but with a gap (now containing a play house but formerly

The vast hollow of the Bowthorpe oak. In the eighteenth century a door was cut in the trunk and a floor and benches installed.

BELOW

One of over a hundred ancient oaks in Windsor Great Park.

a calf shed) of 8 ft/2.4 m separating the two remaining fragments of trunk, although measuring some 44 ft/13.4 m in girth; and the 'Billy Wilkins' in Dorset, said to measure 39½ ft/12 m around its trunk, which is covered with burrs.

Probably the most famous ancient oak in the British Isles, however, is the Major oak, which stands in Sherwood Forest in Nottinghamshire and takes its name from the local antiquary Major Hayman Rooke. Although neither the biggest nor the oldest oak, local people feel that it is very special indeed. Possibly the result of pollarding, and with some of its widest branches supported by 10 ft/3 m posts, it is a very grand old tree, measuring 11 ft/3.37 m in diameter in 1990. Alan Mitchell believed it to be only 480 years old, but according to David Alderman of the Tree Register fo the British Isles, 'because of its time spent within a forest competing with other trees and the number of times it may have been pollarded … its age could be greater than its size suggests.' It was beneath – some people say inside – this tree that the legendary Robin Hood (c. 1250–c. 1350), defender of the poor, is said to have met with his 'merry men'. If this was indeed the case, the Major oak would have had to have reached a good size by the thirteenth century, making the tree possibly around 1,000 years old today.

*S*till let the massy ruin, like the bones of some *majestic hero be preserved unviolated and revered.*

J. G. STRUTT, 'SYLVA BRITANNICA', 1822

The tree commonly known as William the Conqueror's oak, meanwhile, is one of over a hundred ancient pollarded oaks, known affectionately by their traditional name of 'dodders', which still stand in the Great Park of Windsor Castle and date from the Middle Ages. Today it measures 27 ft/8.2 m round and has an enormous hollow in its trunk, said to have been large enough, in 1829, for twenty people to stand in, or twelve to 'sit comfortably down to dinner'. A tree known as Herne the Hunter's oak, also in Windsor Great Park and dating from the thirteenth century, was mourned by Queen Victoria when it was blown down in 1863. Herne the Hunter was an oak god of southern Britain, whose spirit, with horns like antlers, was said to haunt Windsor Forest.

EUROPE'S MOST ANCIENT OAKS

It is certain that in the past some truly colossal oaks existed in other parts of Europe. Ancient oaks still standing fall largely into two main categories: those with enormous boles (generally the result of pollarding) and mostly hollow, or tall individuals with very big trunks, which have not been pollarded.

In France we find the Chêne du Tronjoli – said to be nearly 1,000 years old – which stands on a farm in Brittany. With a magnificent spreading crown and a bole, which has split into two parts, measuring 12¾ ft/3.6 m in diameter (or a combined circumference of 41⅓ ft/12.6 m), it has been suggested that this is possibly the widest bole of any oak in continental Europe. Possibly contemporaneous with it, the exact age of the

Allouville-Bellefosse oak, near Yvetot, is not known. However, it has been a place of devotion for about 300 years – its massive hollow trunk (which measures 12½ ft/3.8 m across) having had a chapel and a hermit's refuge cut into it.

The largest and possibly the oldest oak in Germany (still alive, though very decayed) is to be found in the village of Erle, near Raesfeld in Westphalia. It is known as the Fehme Eiche, or Trial oak, since public meetings and trials were at one time held beneath it. This oak's age has been put, by some, at 1,500 years. Near the village of Ivenack, north of Berlin, a grove of majestic oaks still stands. The trunk of the largest tree ascends for 25 ft/7.6 m before the first branch occurs and measures 12 ft/3.6 m thick at breast height. This tree rivals the largest in Britain, and a sign nearby claims that it is 1,200 years old.

Denmark, France, Sweden, Russia, Herze-govina and Bosnia are all contenders for the country able to boast the oldest oaks in Europe – in fact, the oldest in the world. Two that are still alive in Denmark are said locally to be nearly 2,000 years old. Standing in the forest of Nord-skoven, a remnant of the great forest that once covered much of northern Europe, is the Kongeegen, or Royal oak. Although it has a severely decayed trunk, it still supports a few living branches. According to Canadian tree expert Al Carder, who launched an investigation into the giant trees of the world in 1977, this tree must have had a bole of at least 12 ft/3.6 m in diameter at one time. Slightly smaller, but still very ancient, the oak known as Snoegen, or the 'twisted one' is found nearby.

Although the real age of our most ancient oaks may come to be revised, the myths and legends that have grown up around them look set to remain for many generations to come.

The weathered remains of the Cowthorpe oak in South Yorkshire.

SWEET CHESTNUT

Tree of Protection

BOTANICAL NAME
Castanea sativa

•

DISTRIBUTION
Southern Europe, western Asia, North Africa.

•

OLDEST KNOWN LIVING SPECIMEN
The Tree of One Hundred Horses, Sicily:
recorded in 1770 to have a bole measuring 204 ft/62 m
in girth. Today, the two largest remaining pieces
measure 18 ft/6 m in diameter at 3 ft/1 m from
the ground. Estimated age: 2,000–4,000 years.

•

MYTHICAL SIGNIFICANCE
The Tree of One Hundred Horses is believed to
have sheltered the Queen of Aragon and her retinue
of 100 cavaliers from a rainstorm in 1308.

I
N 1308 GIOVANNA, QUEEN OF ARAGON was on her way to view Mount Etna, Sicily's famous volcano, when she was surprised by a sudden rainstorm. Luckily for her and her escort of 100 cavaliers, they found themselves in the vicinity of a most extra-ordinary tree – one that was already famous for its colossal proportions and was apparently old at the time of Plato, the Greek philosopher (*c.* 428–348 BC), some 1,700 years previously. The tree was a sweet chestnut (*Castanea sativa*) and so huge was its canopy of leaves and branches that Queen Giovanna and her entire retinue – so the legend goes – were able to shelter beneath it. This incident gave rise to the name by which this tree – which still survives in part – is known today: Castagno dei Cento Cavalli or Tree of One Hundred Horses.

THE COLOSSUS OF SICILY

Situated near the village of Sant'Alfio, on the eastern slopes of Mount Etna, at about 1,800 ft/550 m above sea-level, the Tree of One Hundred Horses is considered to be the largest tree – in stoutness, at least – ever recorded. In 1770 its bole was found to be an astonishing 204 feet (68m) in girth. Like Europe's most ancient limes, oaks and yews, this chestnut had also become hollow in extreme old age. In 1670 the hollow was apparently so large that flocks of sheep were penned inside it. Some time later a local family was also reported to be living inside this massive tree.

A B O V E

The Tree of One Hundred Horses in

Sicily, as depicted in 1784.

O P P O S I T E

The massive canopy of the Tree of One

Hundred Horses rises in front of the

smoking volcano of Mount Etna.

Although by this time the chestnut had the appearance of a group of trees growing together, excavations carried out over 200 years ago showed that all the parts were joined to a single root. By 1865 the tree had split into five distinct sections, of which today three separate pieces survive, 12–15 ft/3.5–4.5 m apart. Though damaged, this once-gargantuan chestnut – when in full leaf – still looks very much alive.

It would appear that the sweet chestnut's general decline (over the last few hun-dred years) has been provoked largely by the activities of people, within or around it. While the Tree of One Hundred Horses has recently been fenced, to protect what remains, an engraving dated 1784 clearly shows a dwelling of some sort inside the tree, with pack animals tethered outside. One such hut was fitted with a kiln for drying the sweet

that the mythical dragon Fafnir lived for ninety years in the ground, for ninety years in 'the desert' and ninety more in a lime tree, and there seems to be an interesting ancient connection between dragons and the lime. The legendary German hero Horny Siegfried or Sigurd apparently acquired his name after he had slain Fafnir and bathed himself in its blood. It was after this feat that he became horny and invincible all over, except for one spot between his shoulders to which a lime leaf had stuck. In the German language, an old poetic term for dragon is Lindwurm, which translates as 'lime tree serpent' – perhaps the lime tree was once feared and revered as the haunt of mythical beasts.

EUROPE'S ANCIENT LIMES

Many of the ancient and enormous limes of Europe are broad- or large-leaved limes (*Tilia platyphyllos*). Along with its sister species, the small-leaved lime (*Tilia cordata*),it belongs to the genus Tilia; this comprises some forty-three other species, five of them native to Europe. The broad-leaved lime is the first of the three species to flower (in late June), generally producing three to five large, pale-yellow flowers hanging from a whitish-green bract. With a natural range that extends right across Europe from northern Spain and Sweden, east to the Crimea, the Caucasus and Asia Minor, broad-leaved limes have been widely planted in European parks and gardens, and also as street trees in towns, sometimes forming elegant avenues.

With an impressive crown that forms a towering dome of radiating branches in maturity, the large-leaved lime is regarded as a very shapely tree, capable of reaching giant size, considerable height and very great age. In Lithuania and Poland large, majestic old limes, whose branches may form a canopy over 100 ft/30 m up from the ground, make up a large component of the ancient, wild forests, such as the famous Bialowieza Forest. France is also noted for some remarkable giant limes, such as the Estry lime in Calvados, Normandy (said to be 2,000 years old), but it is in Germany that many of the most outstanding ancient individuals are to be seen.

A huge 1,000-year-old tree, some 100 ft/30 m tall with a wide-spreading canopy, is growing in the Bavarian town of Hoffeld. Almost as tall is the magnificent tree known as the Hindenburg Linde, which stands just a few yards from the Alpenstrasse, above the village of Ramsau in southeast Bavaria. This tree is about 85 ft/26 m in height, has a trunk 38 ft/11.5 m in circumference, a beautiful, broad-spreading crown, and is also believed to be about 1,000 years old.

*Comes sudden on my heart, and I am glad
As I myself were there! Nor in this bower,
This little lime-tree bower, have I not marked
Much that has soothed me. Pale beneath the blaze
Hung the transparent foliage; and I watched
Some broad and sunny leaf, and loved to see
The shadow of the leaf and stem above
Dappling its sunshine!*

SAMUEL TAYLOR COLERIDGE (1772–1834), 'THIS LIME-TREE BOWER MY PRISON'

Another ancient Bavarian lime tree, the Tassilo Linde, thought to be at least 1,200 years old, is to be found in the village of Wessobrunn. An enormous tree, its hollow trunk measures 44 ft/13.3 m in circumference at breast height. In the eighth century it formed part of the wildwood, or *Urwald*, that covered the region, and appears already to have been a large, impressive individual at that time. It is recorded that beneath this tree Duke Tassilo III lay down to sleep after hunting in the surrounding forest. As he slept, he dreamt that he saw three springs, whose waters flowed together in the form of a cross, and that above this spot a Jacob's ladder appeared, with angels climbing up and down it. On waking from his dream, Duke Tassilo asked his hunting guides to look for the springs he had dreamt of. A guide named Wezzo (after whom Wessobrunn is named), found the spot and it was here, in 753, that the Duke decided to found a Benedictine monastery, which, with its baroque and rococo works of art, is well known today. The Tassilo Linde is only a few minutes' walk from the monastery and has now become a place of pilgrimage.

Other impressive ancient limes in Germany, which have a trunk circumference of 52 ft/16 m or more, include the tree at Heede, and the trees at Kötzting and Kasberg, both in Bavaria. According to the German publication *Unsere Baumveteranen* ('Our Tree Veterans'), twenty trees are listed as having reached at least 1,000 years old. One of these is the lime at Upstedt, near Bockenem in Niedersachsen, said to have been planted in AD 850. The tree that is now possibly the widest of any species in Germany is a huge lime growing at Staffelstein in Bavaria. Some 82 ft/25 m in height, its trunk is 79 ft/24 m in circumference – making it one of the broadest-trunked trees in Europe.

In England, the occurrence of large-leaved limes (which arrived from Europe with their small-leaved relatives about 8,000 years ago) is much more restricted than it is in Germany. However, some enormous specimens are still to be found. Probably the most famous is the striking tree growing at Pitchford Hall in Shropshire, which proudly supports a restored eighteenth-century tea house – replacing one from the seventeenth century – among its giant limbs. Measuring about 24 ft/7 m in girth and with branches that are some 8 ft/2.4 m round, this tree certainly looks at least 1,000 years old.

The small-leaved lime is also to be seen in European parks and gardens. Confusingly, its attractive leaves are often bigger than its large-leaved relative. This tree was once very important in lowland England and Europe. Discoveries of preserved pollen and fossilized bark-beetles that feed only on lime show that it played a major role in shaping Europe's native woods. Indeed, it dominated the original wildwood over a large area of the English lowlands and the central European plain for over 2,000 years, after the last Ice Age.

COPPICING, POLLARDING AND IMMORTALITY

The enormous width of many lime trunks and, indeed, the very great ages that these trees can reach has been discovered to be largely due to the ancient practices of pollarding and coppicing. While a pollarded tree is one whose trunk has been cut at around 8–18 ft/2.5–5.5 m, leaving a permanent, broad trunk or 'boll' beneath, a coppiced tree is cut near ground level, leaving a low base or 'stool'. Both methods stimulate the production of new shoots, which are also cut when they have reached the right size.

The practice of coppicing has produced what appears to be the oldest lime yet recorded anywhere in the world. It is a small-leaved lime growing at Westonbirt Arboretum in Gloucestershire which is believed to be a staggering 6,000 years old. The coppice stool was measured to be all of 52 ft/16 m across, and had eighty individual trunks rising from it, before it was cut through for analysis by radiocarbon-dating.

Today the existence of ancient coppiced or pollarded limes in woodland is considered to be a good indication that this woodland is very old – indeed, directly descended from the wildwood of old. The ancient wild limes in Britain's woodlands are not, however, the towering trees of majestic proportions still to be found in undisturbed woods elsewhere in Europe (such as France, Poland and Lithuania) and this has led to their ancient status often being overlooked. History shows us that lime trees have been important to people throughout Europe for thousands of years. It is interesting to reflect that ancient woodland management techniques, performed in the right way and at the right time, actually prolong the life of the tree; indeed, they would seem to make it almost immortal.

BELOW

Part of the giant coppiced, small-leaved lime tree in England that has been radiocarbon-dated at more than 6,000 years old.

OLIVE

Tree of Peace

BOTANICAL NAME
Olea europaea

•

DISTRIBUTION
All countries bounding the Mediterranean;
also cultivated in other warm temperate
or sub-tropical regions.

•

OLDEST KNOWN LIVING SPECIMEN
Some trees in the Garden of Gethsemane and on the
French Riviera believed to be about 2,000 years old.

•

MYTHICAL ASSOCIATIONS
Sacred to the early peoples of the Near East, to the
Egyptians, Greeks and Romans. Believed by the Greeks
to be a gift from the goddess Athena, and by the
Romans to be linked with the goddess Minerva.

OF THE WORLD'S MOST VENERABLE and ancient trees, perhaps none is more closely associated with the history of humankind and the development of Western civilization than the olive. Sacred to the Greeks, Romans and Egyptians, and revered by the early Semitic peoples of the Bible lands, the olive tree has for thousands of years been central to the religion, cultural life, economy and cuisine of millions of people in the Mediterranean region. A source of both food and valuable oil, the olive has an extraordinary ability to renew itself from destruction or decay by producing new shoots and roots; this greatly influenced those peoples in ancient times to regard it as sacred, and to celebrate its significance in myth and legend.

To the ancient Greeks, the olive was a gift from Athena, the goddess of wisdom and the daughter of Zeus, who struck the rock of the Acropolis with her spear and created the first olive tree. In so doing she won the gods' favour, and hence control of the city of Athens (which was named in her honour) from the powerful god Poseidon. Every year the festival of Athena was celebrated as a public holiday, during which olive branches were carried to the Acropolis. At the Olympic Games, the ancient Greek athletic festival held at Olympia, vases filled with sacred olive oil were given as prizes, while the victors wore olive wreaths.

To the Romans, the olive was sacred to Minerva, the goddess of health and wisdom, and it was she who taught the art of olive cultivation. In Egyptian mythology it was Isis, wife of Osiris, who held the secret of teaching the cultivation and use of olives. In Islam, the olive became the Tree of Blessing, giving to the world the light of Allah.

Although its botanical name (*Olea europaea*) suggests a European origin, the olive is actually thought to have been a native of western Asia – perhaps from the region of Mesopotamia, Syria or

OLIVE BRANCHES — SYMBOLS OF PEACE

'And the dove came in to him in the evening; and, lo, in her mouth was an olive leaf pluckt off …' (Genesis 8:11). Ever since the return of the dove to Noah's Ark with an olive leaf in her beak, the dove and the olive have been used in the Christian world as symbols of friendship and peace. In Graeco-Roman symbolism, olive branches also signified well-being and achievement. The Romans continued this tradition by presenting olive crowns to victorious soldiers on their return from battle.

LEFT

Olive fruit have comprised one of the most important harvests for Mediterranean people for thousands of years.

Palestine. Fossilized leaves, dating back to 37,000 BC, have been found on the Aegean island of Santorini, and archaeological evidence suggests that the tree was first domesticated in eastern Mediterranean countries some 10,000 years ago.

Taxonomists have not yet agreed on the ancestry of the cultivated olive. Some believe it to be descended from the wild olive (*O. oleaster*), or from the more widespread *O. chrysophylla*. Others believe that the original olive was *O. europaea* after all. It seems likely, however, that careful tending and experimentaton by generations of prehistoric people – who discover-

ABOVE

Cloths are often spread beneath olive trees like these in southern Italy to collect the fruit.

ed that olive shoots could be grafted and replanted – refined and encouraged the tree's productivity. With careful pruning and the right environment (hot summers, but winters cold enough to set the fruit), the olive tree could be nurtured to yield superior fruit.

A PRECIOUS RESOURCE

The olive was undoubtedly one of the most valuable trees of the ancient Hebrews, and the Bible abounds with references to it. In Psalm 128, for example, the trees become a symbol of prosperity and plenty, and of divine blessing: 'Happy are those who obey the Lord, … your sons will be like olive trees around your table.' And among medieval Christians many myths also grew up concerning the olive.

In ancient times the religious and ceremonial uses of olive oil were highly significant. In the scriptures and in Classical writings, olive oil is referred to as an emblem of goodness and purity, and it may have been this oil that formed the base for the 'ointment of spikenard' used to anoint Jesus' feet before the Last Supper. In biblical times olive oil was also regarded as an emblem of sovereignty, and it played an important role in coronation ceremonies. Saul, the first King of Israel, was crowned by rubbing oil into his forehead. Olive oil was further used in the preparation of sacrificial offerings, in funeral rites, perfumes and cosmetics, and as an aid to healing.

As has been pointed out by experts on the plants used at that time, the general references to 'gardens' in the Bible are often references to olive orchards or groves.

century AD such groves were to be found at the fringes of the entire Mediterranean, across southern Europe and in North Africa.

The beauty of the olive tree has been extolled in works of art for thousands of years. Images of the trees or fruit have been depicted in Minoan frescos, on Grecian pottery jars, Roman silver vases and in countless friezes and carvings of the ancient world.

THE IMMORTAL OLIVE

With their lance-shaped, evergreen leaves – a deep grey-green above and silvery white on the underside – and the gnarled grey trunks that develop in old age, olive trees form one of the most characteristic aspects of Mediterranean vegetation. Though they may reach about 49 ft/15 m in height, olives are generally small trees and in some areas (such as Provence, Greece and Cyprus) they are pollarded at 16-23 ft/5-7 m to improve the crop and to make harvesting easier.

The murmur of an olive grove has something very intimate, immensely old. It is too beautiful for me to try to conceive of it or dare to paint it.

VINCENT VAN GOGH (1853–90)

Believed by some experts to be able to live for over 1,500 years, the olive tree shares with the yew, small-leaved lime and sweet chestnut the distinction of being among Europe's oldest trees. Pliny the Elder (AD 23–79), the Roman naturalist and chronicler, recorded that the Athenians venerated a tree that they claimed was 1,600 years old.

The olive matures very slowly and may need several decades to reach full maturity and productivity. Its crop is not said to diminish until some 150 years have been reached, but long after this it is still capable of bearing a good harvest. Pliny refers to an olive grove that was still producing fruit, though over 700 years old. In old age, olive trees become grotesquely gnarled, in wonderful contrast to their light, silvery foliage. By about 200 years of age the olive appears truly ancient: its branches and trunk have become twisted and contorted, and shoots develop at its base, which will eventually grow up to form a new tree. Some botanists believe that an individual olive trunk will not live for much longer than about 700 years, but the tree's massive root ball will continue to throw out new shoots for centuries. New roots are also formed when the old roots die.

This tendency, and the tree's ability to produce new shoots, or suckers, which will become a new tree even after the trunk has died or been felled, have given rise to the reputation of the olive as an immortal tree. Even if it were true that the Roman emperor Titus Vespasian (AD 9–79) did – as was reported, by contemporary scholars – cut down the olives growing in the Garden of Gethsemane in AD 70, it would appear that he did not actually kill them!

A slow-growing and tenacious tree, the olive needs very little water. It can search out moisture at great depths, sending its roots down some 20 ft/6 m in search of it. Although olives have evolved to be able to survive on parched, dry soils, they are very responsive to irrigation and fertilization and will produce a heavier and more reliable

OPPOSITE

One of the oldest olives on the island of Cyprus. According to legend, the oldest tree took root from a stone spat out by a visiting disciple.

crop if given this care. But to produce any quantity of useful fruit, the olive is dependent upon human hands in another ways, since the trees require grafting. Trees that grow up from seeds or suckers will produce only small, inferior fruit; they must be budded or grafted onto an established variety to do well. Cuttings are often grafted onto the stumps of old trees. Today, some 700 hundred named varieties – or cultivars – exist.

In early summer olive trees produce a multitude of small, white, perfumed flowers, which appear in groups under the preceding year's leaves. Although they are pollinated by wind, they can be very easily damaged by strong winds, heavy rain and spring frosts, all of which can kill the flowers. Because they are susceptible to a range of environmental factors, the production of fruit is erratic: trees may produce a heavy crop one year and not even bloom the next.

The black and green olives with which we are familiar are not produced by different trees: the olive's fruits are green at first but become a satiny, dark blue or purplish blue-black as they ripen, bursting with yellow oil. In this mature state they cling to the tree for several weeks before falling to the ground. For countless generations of traditional, small-scale farmers olive growing is a special art, requiring patience and skill, an empathy with the trees that could just as well be reserved for people. As one French grower from Provence put it: 'Olive trees respond to man, they interact … There is no more passionate tree anywhere, nothing that relates to man like an olive.'

An interesting belief arose in parts of the Mediterranean that the production of olive fruit was influenced by the moral standing of the picker. Thus, in ancient Greece, for a time only virgins and young men sworn to chastity were allowed to harvest the trees. Until recently, in some parts of Italy, a common tradition also held that

Olive groves are an integral part of many Mediterranean landscapes like this one in southern Italy.

the olive crop was sensitive to virtue. If tended by young, innocent children, the olive yield would be more prolific, but if the farmer was unfaithful to his wife, then his misdemeanours would be reflected in a poor harvest!

Olives have signified land, or rather rights to land, for thousands of years. Many people – such as the Palestinians – feel that their identity is intricately linked to their trees. But today in the Holy Land olive trees have become, sadly, objects of war rather than symbols of peace – trees being destroyed, often as a first move, in battles over land.

THE OLIVE HARVEST

In the Mediterranean region the ancient olive-harvesting process takes place during the autumn and winter months, varying from region to region depending both on climate and the requirements of the grower.

As a general rule, harvesting by hand is still the most common method because it allows the best fruits to be selected for eating as 'table olives', without damaging the trees. In other places the olives are left to fall to the ground naturally; another method, often employed in Italy and Spain, is to use a long pole to beat the trees, or a kind of long-toothed comb may be stroked through the foliage to loosen the fruit. In biblical times, olives were also gathered by shaking or beating the trees, but a few fruit would always be left on them, for the poor, strangers, orphans and widows to gather.

It takes about 11 lb/5 kg of olives to make 1¾ pt/1 litre of oil, most of which comes from the outer flesh of the olive. The simplest and most ancient means of pressing olives dates back over 6,000 years. In the eastern Mediterranean the olives would first be crushed in a mortar and the resulting paste transferred to an earthenware jar. Hot water was then poured over the paste while it was kneaded by hand. As it is lighter than water, the olive oil released from the fruits would float to the surface, allowing it to be skimmed off.

People who live among olive trees talk of the air being purer because of them. When asked on her 121st birthday how she had survived to be the world's oldest woman, Jeanne Calment of Arles, in France, answered simply: 'Olive oil!' And it may be largely as a health-giver that the noble olive tree is revered in the next millennium.

ABOVE

Because olive trees need so little water their wood is extremely hard and was much used in the past. It is still prized today for cabinet work and turnery.

The whole Mediterranean, the sculpture, the palms, its gold beads, the bearded heroes, the wine, the ideas, the ships, the moonlight, the winged gorgons, the bronze men, the philosophers – all of it seems to rise in the sour, pungent taste of these black olives … A taste older than meat, older than wine. A taste as old as cold water.

LAWRENCE DURRELL (1912-90), 'PROSPERO'S CELL'

WELWITSCHIA

Dwarf Tree of the Namib Desert

BOTANICAL NAME
Welwitschia mirabilis

•

DISTRIBUTION
The northern gravel plains of the Namib Desert, from
the Kuiseb River to southern Angola.

•

OLDEST KNOWN LIVING SPECIMEN
Carbon-dating of the largest Namibian trees indicates
that they are more than 2,000 years old.

NAMED AFTER THE AUSTRIAN-BORN doctor and botanist Friedrich Welwitsch (1807–72), who in 1859 was the first European to discover this bizarre plant, *Welwitschia mirabilis* is now known to exist only on the gravel plains of the northern Namib Desert, from the Kuiseb River to southern Angola. In some areas, such as Swakopmund, welwitschias exist in large numbers and form the dominant vegetation.

The ancestry of the welwitschia is thought to be extremely ancient and it is regarded as a 'living fossil' – a link with the prehistoric flora of the super-continent Gondwana-land that existed millions of years ago. Its form and proportions are so unusual that there is nothing else comparable in the plant kingdom. It is so unlike any other plant that it is a unique species, occupying its own genus.

The name given to the tree by the Topnaar, who live in the western central Namib Desert, is *otji-tumbo*, or 'Mr Big', while the Afrikaners have more recently dubbed it *tweeblaarkanniedood*, or 'two-leaves cannot die'.

The 'trunk' of the welwitschia takes the form of an inverted cone, like a giant parsnip, which is almost entirely buried under the sand. This trunk, which can reach a girth of 4 ft/1.2 m or more, rarely rises more than 3 ft/1 m above the ground, but tapers into a tap root that penetrates some 10 ft/3 m down beneath the desert. Although primarily a water-storage organ, the trunk is reported to be as hard as the hardest wood and covered in a corrugated cork-like bark.

From the subterranean trunk, a crown of dishevelled foliage spreads out across the arid desert surface. This typically appears as a mound of vegetation torn to tatters by the desert wind. Strangely, the adult plant bears just a single pair of leathery leaves, which emerge from deep grooves on opposite sides of the broad, squat 'trunk', with a pronounced crater in the centre. The leaves, which are greenish-brown in colour, can grow to a staggering 6 ft/1.8 m in length in old trees, and are the only ones ever produced during its entire lifetime – which may extend to thousands of years. As the leaves develop, they become broad, leathery and heavily ribbed; over time they are torn into narrow ribbons by the fierce desert winds. These ribbons become twisted, bent and entangled and lie in tattered heaps on either side of the crown.

Of all the strange and wonderful ancient trees around the world, perhaps the welwitschia is the species that looks most like an extra-terrestrial form of life. Half-buried in the sands of the lunar landscape of the Namib Desert, it is unlike any other tree. In fact, the first European ever to set eyes on a welwitschia thought the vision so unlikely that he was afraid to reach out and touch it, fearing that it was simply a mirage.

Everything about the welwitschia is curious, including its flowering habit. Trees are either male or female – the male trees have erect scarlet cones that rise about 12 in/30 cm above the trunk, and 'flowers' that sprout from the scale of the cones. The pollen is conveyed to the reddish cones of the female trees by insects. Once pollinated, the females produce small winged seeds that are dispersed by the wind. These can lie dormant in the sand or in rocky crevices for many years before germinating.

ANCIENT SURVIVORS OF THE NAMIB DESERT

The welwitschias are true survivors. Not only do they thrive in the demanding environment of the Namib Desert, but recent research has shown that they can live for thousands of years as well. Tests carried out on welwitschias using carbon-14 dating

ABOVE

This ancient welwitschia is estimated to be over 1,500 years old, yet stands only 5 ft/1.5 m tall.

techniques have established the age of some of the trees. Certain larger individuals, with trunks measuring over 3¼ ft/1 m at the crown, were found to be more than 2,000 years old, while even those of modest size were over 700 years old.

The very great age that the welwitschia may reach, like many other ancient tree species, may be part of its long-term survival strategy. It may be that climatic cycles are in operation in western Africa that are measured in hundreds, if not thousands, of years. Undoubtedly, in the past, parts of Africa enjoyed far more rain than they do today, so it may be the case that the welwitschia is adapted to a cycle of climatic variation that is on too grand a scale for us to perceive.

Since rain is absent in the desert for three out of every four years, the welwitschia has become adapted to maximize and conserve the little water that is available. Early researchers noted the long tap root and believed that it penetrated deep into the ground to draw up underground water. However, recent research has revealed that while the tap root is important during the four-yearly rains, the plant has developed a more ingenious way of collecting water. The welwitschia grows in part of the Namib Desert that is subject to dense sea fogs all year round, and it is the condensation of the fog and the heavy dews that provide the tree with its water. The specially adapted pores on the leaves trap the precious moisture from the air, while the tangle of torn leaves enables the water to be channelled onto the sand, so that it can be absorbed by its roots.

Another of the welwitschia's survival strategies is to make itself unpalatable to grazing animals. The leaves and bark contain bitter compounds that deter most predators, although the black rhino has been known to eat the welwitschia from time to time. The tree also exudes a colourless resin from its leaves and stem, which protects it against most insects and diseases. However, the dwarf tree's most prominent inhabitant is the yellow-and-black pyrrhcorid bug (*Probergrothius sexpunctatis*), which has found a way round the welwitschia's defences and lives by sucking its sap. Even sticking its head in the sand has not enabled this ancient survivor totally to avoid detection by predators.

One curious aspect of the welwitschia's botany is the ability of several plants living close together to fuse into larger 'graft complexes'. The English botanist H.H.W. Pearson wrote in 1909:

'Of three such united groups, one consisted of a solid mass of five plants – one male and four female. One of the female plants, occupying a central position, appeared as if longitudinally split from the crown downwards by the ingrowth of another. A second clump contained two females at least: they were so intimately united that details of individuals could not be made out. In a third group, the largest of the three, the number of constituent plants was quite indeterminable. Apparently the second group contained no males, while the third was made up entirely of males.'

The welwitschia has adapted to the harsh environment of the Namib Desert, which receives less that 1¼ in/3 cm of rain each year.

ABOVE AND RIGHT

The male flowers (above) produce a red pollen, which is transferred to the female flowers (right) by insects. When fully ripe, the seeds of the female cones are dispersed by the wind.

BAOBAB

Upside-Down Tree

BOTANICAL NAME
Adansonia digitata and other species

•

DISTRIBUTION
A. digitata: most of the African continent and
Madagascar; Madagascar only: *A. grandidieri, A.
madagascariensis, A. perieri, A. rubrostipa, A. suarezensis, A.
za*; northern Australia only: *A. gregorii*.

•

OLDEST KNOWN LIVING SPECIMEN
The largest baobab is in Northern Province:
45 ft/ 13.7m in diameter. Estimated to be at least
3,000 years old.

•

RELIGIOUS SIGNIFICANCE
Considered holy in some places, and to
be the home of important spirits.

•

MYTHICAL ASSOCIATIONS
Numerous, relating to its origin (how it came to
be the upside-down tree) and its powers.

•

CONSERVATION STATUS
All the species native to Madagascar are threatened.

R ISING OUT OF THE SAVANNAH GRASSES with its broad, grotesque trunk and squat stature, Africa's most famous and distinctive tree – the baobab – is an arresting sight. Often wider than it is high, and with root-like branches that are devoid of leaves for large parts of the year, the 'upside-down tree' (as it is sometimes affectionately known) seems an entirely appropriate name for this curiosity.

First described by a European in 1592, in Prospero Alpini's *De plantis Aegypti liber* ('Natural History of Egypt'), the most common species of baobab, *Adansonia digitata*, astonished viewers over 400 years ago. Growing over a large proportion of the African continent, this baobab – which is also known as Judas' bag and the monkey-bread tree – occurs as far north as Sudan and as far south as Northern Province in South Africa, and from the Cape Verde Islands in the west to Ethiopia and Madagascar in the east. Altogether there are eight species of baobab: six of them occur only on the island of Madagascar, while one other species grows only in northern Australia.

The largest authenticated baobab alive today stands at Sagole in the Norther Province and measures an astounding 45 ft/13.7 m in diameter. Some experts now believe that it is entirely possible that trees of over 50 ft/15.25 m have existed in the past. In fact the Scottish missionary and explorer David Livingstone (1813–73) once camped under a baobab that was 85 ft/26 m in circumference, and there are still many trees with girths greater than 32 ft/10 m. An interesting feature of the baobab, which can make the recording of its precise dimensions more challenging, is that its trunk may fluctuate in size between seasons, as water is stored or used up.

The French botanist Michel Adanson (1727–1806) ascribed ages to some of the trees he had seen that were considered by many to be sacrilegious. His greatest estimate for an individual tree was 6,000 years. This implied that it must have begun life before the great Flood of the Old Testament, then commonly believed to have taken place only 4,000 years before. Most scientists of the time disagreed with Adanson's calculations, but recent studies of tree rings and carbon-dated material taken from living trees have shown that baobabs can indeed live to very great ages. A tree with a girth of just 14¾ ft/4.5 m, for example, has been shown to be over 1,000 years old. While the exact ages of most of the greatest baobabs of Africa have not been calculated, estimates based on the above

A Caliban of a tree, a grizzled, distorted old goblin with the girth of a giant, the hide of a rhinoceros, twiggy fingers clutching at empty air.

HILARY BRADT, 'GUIDE TO MADAGASCAR'

OPPOSITE

The most noticeable feature of the baobab is not its height or the size of its crown, but the enormous thickness of its trunk.

ABOVE

The massive trunk of the baobab at
Sagole in South Africa is 45 ft/ 13.7 m
in diameter. This is probably the tree with
the widest trunk in the world.

information point to ages of more than 4,000 years for some. Research into the ages of the boab tree of Australia (*A. gregorii*) suggests that they can also reach ages in excess of 2,000 years. The Madagascan species have been less studied, so their ages can only be guessed at. However, we know – from studies of the great ages reached by bristlecone pines, for instance – that challenging growing conditions can produce trees of great age, if not great size, and thus some relatively small baobabs could still be immensely old.

The botany of Africa's most common baobab (*A. digitata*) is fascinating. It is not usually a tall tree, reaching only 45–75 ft/14–23 m in height, but it is famous for its gigantic girth. The main trunk is generally cylindrical in shape and suddenly tapers into a number of comparatively small, thin, spreading branches. Baobabs are deciduous trees and new foliage usually appears in late spring or early summer. The leaves of *A. digitata* take the form of five to seven leaflets, which look like fingers on a hand, giving rise to its botanical term *digitata*. They have large, sweet-scented white flowers, some 5–7 in/ 13–18 cm wide, which are pollinated by a variety of nocturnal creatures, including bats and bushbabies. The egg-shaped fruits are covered with a green velvety substance, which makes them look rather like velvet purses dangling from the branches. The thick, woody shell of the fruit encases a pulpy white flesh in which a number of black seeds are set. This edible fruit is particularly relished by baboons, and this has given rise to one of the baobab's popular names: monkey-bread tree.

TREE OF LIFE

To many of the native peoples of Africa the baobab has not simply been a familiar feature of the savannah landscape but, literally, a 'tree of life'. It is the baobab's special ability to store water during droughts that has enabled many settled communities and nomadic peoples to survive, even though they may be far from any river system. Over thousands of years the distribution of these strange trees has facilitated the expansion of great African nations, such as the Bantu.

The baobab has an enormous trunk that acts as a water-storage organ: the largest baobabs can contain more than 30,000 gallons/136,000 litres of water. Many African peoples learnt long ago how to make use of this all-important feature. The Kalahari bushmen, for example, use the hollow stems of grasses joined together, like straws, to reach the water inside the trunk, from where it can be sucked out. In Sudan, however, some large baobab trunks are deliberately hollowed out so that they will collect rainwater during the rainy season.

The baobab is remarkable not only for its water-storing properties; it also provides a number of very useful products that have become central to the way of life of numerous people. Once the bark has been cut away from the trunk, an inner bast layer is revealed that yields a strong fibre used for making ropes, sacks and nets, and it is even woven to make cloth. Other uses include the strings for musical instruments and waterproof hats. Fortunately, baobabs have a remarkable ability to regenerate and can survive the removal of large areas of bark.

A TREE THAT FIGHTS FEVERS

Baobabs have a long history of use, over thousands of years, for medicinal purposes. In Africa their bark is still used for the treatment of fevers and, for a time in Europe, it was used in place of cinchona bark (the source of quinine) in order to fight malaria. Because they are rich in vitamin C and calcium, the leaves and fruit also act in a preventative capacity against certain illnesses. And in parts of Africa baobab pulp is burnt so that the smoke will fumigate the insects that live on domestic cattle.

LEFT

The leaves and pulp of the baobab fruit also contain compounds that suppress fevers and these have often been put to use to combat dysentery.

PREVIOUS PAGE

A baobab growing among the giant boulders at the foot of the Bandiagara Escarpment in Mali.

BELOW

The weekly market in the Dogon village of Tireli in Mali takes place beneath ancient baobabs.

In Africa the egg-shaped fruits of the baobab are an important source of nutrition. The woody shell encloses seeds set in a fleshy pulp, both of which can be eaten. The pulp has a pleasant, tart flavour and, when dried, can be mixed with water to make a refreshing drink. The fruit contains citric and tartaric acids, which are important to the diet of nomadic peoples. These acids have also been used by herding peoples in Africa to coagulate milk, and commercially to coagulate rubber.

The baobab's seeds – which are high in protein and oil – are generally either eaten on their own or mixed with millet to form a kind of gruel. They may also be pounded into a paste, like peanut-butter, or traded for the extraction of their oil. Other parts of

the tree that are edible include the young shoots put out by germinating seedlings, which are eaten like asparagus. Young leaves are also sometimes used in salads and provide important fodder for domesticated and wild animals alike. In Northern Province, caterpillars that live on the baobabs are also gathered as a food by the local people.

The trunk of the baobab tends to become hollow with old age, but in some areas people have assisted nature by hollowing out the trees themselves. Many ancient trees have considerable cavities of this kind inside them and, over the centuries, some extra-ordinary and ingenious uses have been made of this feature. The hollow inside the tree has proved to be an ideal place to store grain, water or even livestock, while in larger baobabs people have even been known to set up home. In Senegal, many hollows have been used as municipal buildings, sometimes with the badges of office carved into the outer trunk.

Today a tree, reputed to be possibly up to 6,000 years old, has been fitted out inside as a bar, complete with draught-beer taps and a fridge. It is still in use on a farm near Duiwelskloof, in the Northern Province, and can hold fifty-six people at any one time.

B E L O W

The fibrous bast layer under the baobab's bark is useful for making rope and baskets.

MYTHS AND LEGENDS

It is not surprising that a tree of such imposing stature as the baobab, and one that has become so important to so many different cultures, should have become the focus of numerous myths, legends and superstitions. A large number of beliefs about the baobab were collected by anthropologists and explorers at the beginning of the twentieth century. In both east and west Africa it was noted that mischievous spirits were believed to reside in the trees. In the Northern Province of South Africa, for example, it is still believed by some that spirits inhabit the large, white flowers and that anyone who plucks them will be eaten by a lion. In Senegal and Gambia, a tradition of placing the dead bodies of poets, musicians and 'buffoons' inside baobabs was also noted. These people were believed to be possessed by demons and could therefore cause bad luck to befall crops or fisheries, if they were buried in the ground or at sea.

The following legend, of which there are numerous variations, comes from the slopes of Mount Kilimanjaro in Kenya. It relates the story explaining how the baobab came to look as it does today:

'A long, long time ago, a baobab stood beside a little pond and raised up its branches towards the sky. It looked at the other trees, whose crowns were covered in flowers, delicate bark and leaves. They shimmered with colour and the baobab saw all of this in the surface of the pond – like a mirror – and became angry. His own leaves were very small and his flowers scarcely visible. He was fat and his bark resembled the wrinkled skin of an old elephant. The tree called up to God and pleaded with him.

'God had created the baobab and was satisfied with his work because it did not resemble the other trees. He liked diversity. The only thing was, he couldn't bear criticism. He asked the tree if it found the hippopotamus beautiful, and if it liked the cry of the hyena. Then God went back up into the clouds. He wanted to be left alone, to reflect in peace.

'The baobab didn't stop looking at himself in the mirror, or complaining. So God came down again, seized the baobab, lifted him up and replanted him, upside-down in the earth. After this the baobab no longer looked at himself in the mirror, or complained again. Everything was restored to order.'

MADAGASCAN MYSTERY

It is a curious fact that only one baobab species, *Adansonia digitata*, is found across the entire continent of Africa, but the same species and six others are found on the island of Madagascar. The reason for the occurrence of unique Madagascan baobabs remains a mystery. However, it is proposed that, after Madagascar separated from mainland Africa, unusual evolutionary conditions gave rise to the additional six species.

LEFT

The most spectacular of the endemic baobabs is A. grandidieri, known in Malagasy as 'mother of the forest'. This baobab is found only in the flood plain and along river banks in southwest Madagascar, where the Sakalava people value its fruit and seeds.

KAURI

Lord of the Forest

BOTANICAL NAME
Agathis australis

•

DISTRIBUTION
Northern North Island, New Zealand.

•

OLDEST KNOWN LIVING SPECIMEN
Tane Mahuta in Waipoua Forest: estimated age: 2,100
years; total height: 169 ft/51.5 m; girth: 45 ft/13.7 m;
volume: 8,635 cu ft/244.5 cu m.

•

RELIGIOUS SIGNIFICANCE
Believed to possess its own spirit, and revered
by the Maori people of New Zealand
for its great size and strength.

•

MYTHICAL ASSOCIATIONS
Likened by the Maoris to the whale, the master
of the sea, because of its huge dimensions
and the smoothness of its bark.

WITH THEIR MASSIVE COLUMNAR trunks and elegant tracery of branches, the kauri trees of New Zealand give an unmistakable character to the North Island valleys and ridges they once dominated, and have inspired some who observed them to liken them to Gothic cathedrals. Clearly distinct from the other trees that make up the sub-tropical rain forest around them, they rival the giant redwoods of California in size, and the largest individuals alive today are believed to be more than 2,000 years old.

These giants belong to an extremely ancient family of trees, the Araucariaceae, which were abundant before the coming of the dinosaurs and the break-up of the super-continent Gondwanaland. Although there are thirteen other species and two sub-species of kauri, which grow in the tropical regions of Australia, Melanesia, New Guinea, the Philippines, the Celebes, Borneo, Sumatra and the Malay peninsula, the southern kauri (*Agathis australis*) is found only in New Zealand. More distant relatives of the kauri include the monkey puzzle and parana pine of South America and the Norfolk Island pine. In the far north of New Zealand's North Island are swamplands where large kauri trees that were growing some 30–50,000 years ago have been discovered, preserved under water.

Before the arrival of Europeans, kauri forest covered an estimated 4 million acres/1.6 million hectares of New Zealand's North Island. It was Captain Cook's excited reference to the forests he saw in 1769 that attracted the first European timber men. Cook (1728–79) noted:'The banks of the river were completely clothed with the finest timber my eyes have ever seen…'

The arrival of the timber men, however, was to spell disaster both for the kauri trees and for the culture of the Maori people, by whom the trees were revered. What followed was the wholesale destruction of the ancient and majestic kauri forests: in just 150 years they were to shrink to an area of barely 18,420 acres/7,455 hectares.

In the latter half of the twentieth century people have come to appreciate the intrinsic value of the kauri forests once more. Today there are a number of refuges where the remaining giants are protected for posterity. Here it is possible to walk among trees that have been growing for the last 2,000 years and to visit the individual whose

We travelled through a wood so thick that the light of heaven could not penetrate the trees that composed it. Not a gleam of sky was to be seen. All was a mass of gigantic trees, straight and lofty, their wide-spreading branches meeting overhead and producing an endless darkness.

AUGUSTUS EARLE

gigantic proportions have led it to become the best known of all: Tane Mahuta – the Lord of the Forest.

Kauri trees can grow to an immense size. Although the list of 'greatest' trees continues to change, the living tree today estimated to have the broadest trunk is known by its Maori name Te Matua Ngahere, or 'Father of the Forest'. Its trunk is 54 ft/16.4 m in girth and it is free of branches for 33 ft/10.2 m from the ground. The total height of the tree is 98 ft/30 m. However, not far away, also in the Waipoua forest, is Tane Mahuta, the largest standing kauri tree. Despite having a narrower trunk than Te Matua Ngahere – measuring 45 ft/13.7 m in girth – it is much taller: 169 ft/51.5 m, and its massive trunk rises nearly 59 ft/18 m before the first branch appears.

Conservationist Stephen King, who has spent much time studying the ancient kauri forest, recently discovered a 'new' tree, which he has nicknamed 'the phantom kauri',

ABOVE

Young kauri trees in Waipoua Kauri Forest displaying the straight, branchless trunks that made them so attractive to the timbermen of the nineteenth century.

because it was originally discovered in the 1920s, then 'lost' and eventually rediscovered in the 1970s. This tree is now estimated to take second place, in terms of its overall size, after Tane Mahuta, with 59 ft/18 m of clear bole and a circumference of over 39 ft/12 m. It is thought that it could contain as much as 8,475 cu ft/ 240 cu m of timber.

In the past there were kauris that were much larger than the trees which survive today. Tane Mahuta has been estimated to contain some 8,635 cu ft/ 244.5 cu m of timber, but on the slopes of Tutamoe, above Kaihu in Northland, stood a tree known as Kairaru, which was calculated to have contained 15,997 cu ft/

ABOVE

Kauri trees tend to live on nutrient-poor soils, in which small shrubs and hardy grasses form the understorey.

453 cu m of commercial timber before it was destroyed by forest fire in the 1880s. This extraordinary tree was more than three times the size of Tane Mahuta, making it larger in volume than the greatest giant redwoods today and, in its time, the largest tree (by timber volume) recorded in the world. Tane Mahuta is reckoned (by counting the ring sequences from felled trees of equal girth) to be 2,100 years old, but it is possible that Kairaru could have been more than 4,000 years old by the time it was destroyed.

THE KAURI FOREST

New Zealand's kauri forests developed only in the area of North Island which has a warm, sub-tropical climate. Part of the rich and varied community of trees that flourished here, kauri trees did not cover large, continuous areas, but tended to form pockets or groves within the rain forests or coastal forests of the region. These forests held a number of other giant tree species, most notably podocarp species, such as totara (*Podocarpus totara*), rimu (*Dacrydium cupressinum*) and kahikatea (*Dacrycarpus dacrydioides*).

The kauris have developed in association with a number of other tree species, and with vines and shrubs, which form a tangled understorey. Tall grasses, such as astelia and ghania sedge, often form shimmering stands amid the forests, while grass trees, ferns and orchids are also typical. Young kauris sometimes compete with, and eventually overtake, copper-coloured celery pines, at the edges of the forests. The shade cast by the giant kauris as they develop, and the nutrient-poor soils surrounding them, tend to prevent other large trees from becoming established nearby.

OPPOSITE

The distinctive foliage and canopy shape of the kauris can clearly be seen in this view across the North Island's Waipoua Forest.

A curious feature of kauri trees, which are a kind of ancient pine, is that as they develop they change shape, as well as size. As a young 'ricker', in adolescence, the tall, thin-stemmed tree grows rapidly, assuming a narrow, conical shape. As it approaches maturity – at about 100–120 years old – it begins to develop a distinctive crown. Soon after the crown has begun to form, the lower limbs die back and fall off, leaving the smooth grey trunk that typifies an ancient kauri tree. The crown continues to fan out, eventually becoming an immense framework of branches. To support this top-heavy shape, deep tap roots extend for many yards into the ground and develop knob-like structures at the tree's base to provide extra stability.

As the tree reaches a great age – many hundreds of years old – the trunk often becomes hollow, but new roots develop and form a direct link between the crown and

When he [a Maori] enters the forest he is among the offspring of Tane the Fertilizer, from whom he is also descended. He is among his own kindred, the descendants of the elder branch of his family, begotten by their common ancestor Tane, and under his protection. Thus when a man of the younger branch wishes to slay a member of the elder branch – that is to say, when he desires to fell a tree – it is necessary that he should avert ill consequences by a placation of Tane, the progenitor of trees and of man.

ELSDEN BEST, 'THE MAORI CANOE'

the ground by passing down through the inside of the tree. In this way the kauris are able to flourish into old age.

Perhaps the most remarkable feature of the tree is its smooth, grey, branchless trunk – the sides being almost parallel until the branching crown is reached. The kauri has developed an ingenious way of remaining clear of parasitic plants, by simply shedding plates of its mottled bark whenever an unwanted guest tries to attach itself. Conversely, the tree's huge crown supports a number of epiphytic plants, including ferns and orchids.

In order to reproduce, pollen from male catkins must come into contact with the female cones, which are green and about the size of a golf ball. In the autumn, the tiny winged seeds are ejected from the cones while they are still on the tree, but they can survive in this state for only a few days. A few seeds that fall onto suitable soils, in areas

LEFT

Tāne Mahuta is the largest living kauri tree today, but it contains only half the volume of wood of the largest kauri ever recorded.

ABOVE AND RIGHT

The smooth trunk of the kauri regularly sheds flakes of bark (above), so preventing the growth of epiphytes. When damaged, the kauri tree exudes a resinous gum, which congeals in lumps (right) as a defence against fungi and wood-boring insects.

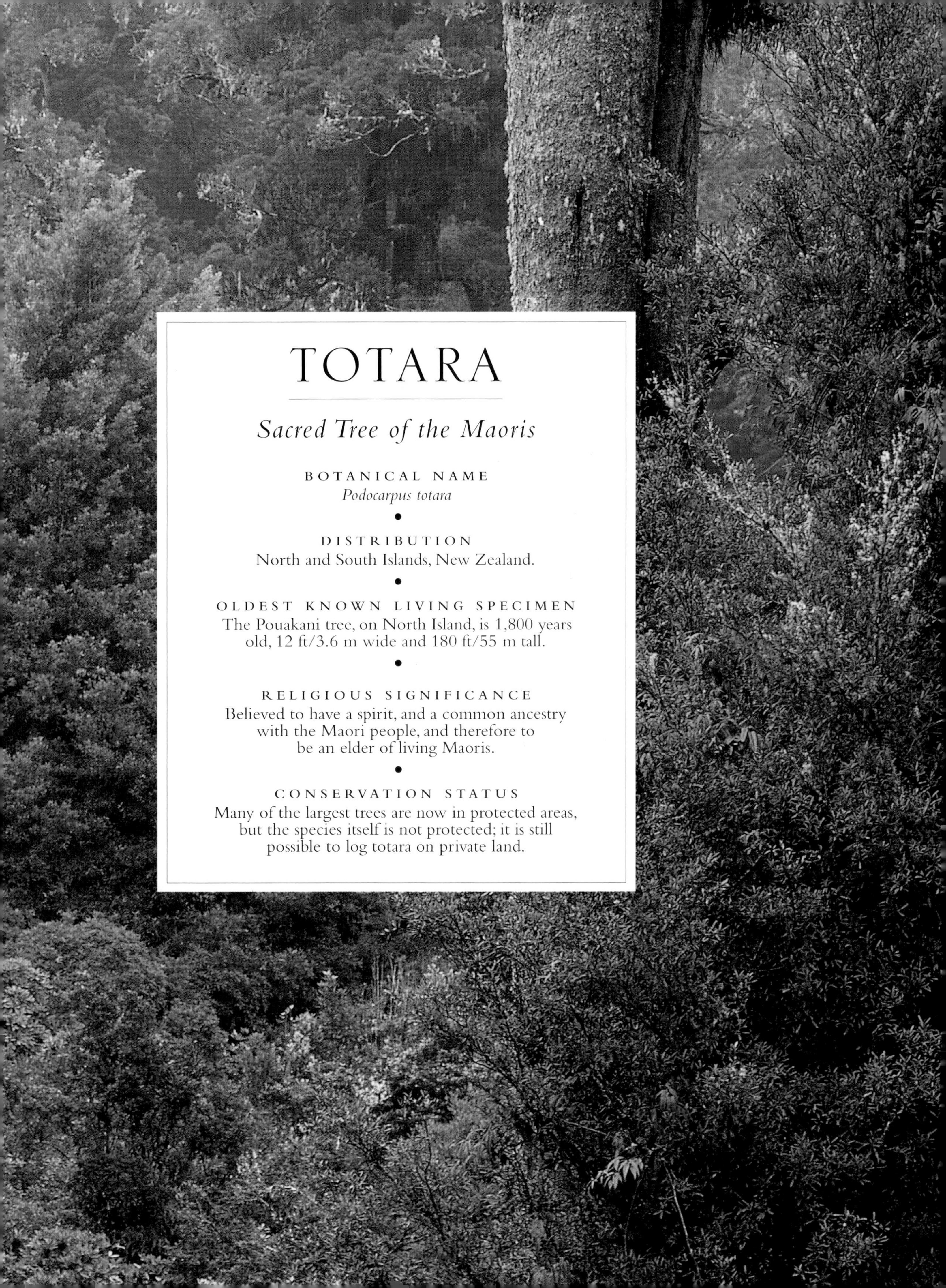

TOTARA

Sacred Tree of the Maoris

BOTANICAL NAME
Podocarpus totara

•

DISTRIBUTION
North and South Islands, New Zealand.

•

OLDEST KNOWN LIVING SPECIMEN
The Pouakani tree, on North Island, is 1,800 years
old, 12 ft/3.6 m wide and 180 ft/55 m tall.

•

RELIGIOUS SIGNIFICANCE
Believed to have a spirit, and a common ancestry
with the Maori people, and therefore to
be an elder of living Maoris.

•

CONSERVATION STATUS
Many of the largest trees are now in protected areas,
but the species itself is not protected; it is still
possible to log totara on private land.

THE TOTARA (*PODOCARPUS TOTARA*) is one of New Zealand's most magnificent and important trees, but is now found growing only in isolated pockets of forest. The Pureora Forest Reserve, which straddles the Hauhungaroa Range, west of Lake Taupo and east of Te Kuiti, is one of this tree's last refuges. Small ferns and bushes form the ground and shrub layers of the forest, while larger trees make up the canopy and sub-canopy. Towering above are the forest giants, such as the totara.

The podocarp, to which the totara belongs, is an extremely ancient tree family, which was thriving long before the islands that comprise New Zealand had separated from the continents of South America, Australasia, Africa and Asia around 150 million years ago. Fossil records show that over the past seventy million years the podocarps of New Zealand have remained virtually unchanged botanically.

The totara tree can attain great age. One of the largest and oldest examples is the tree known as Pouakani, located on the western side of Pureora mountain. With a diameter of 12 ft/ 3.6 m, comparison with felled trees of the same size, whose growth rings have been counted, have led experts to believe that this tree is 1,800 years old. Such investigation of ancient tree stumps has shown that totaras are able to live to beyond 2,000 years old.

THE TREE AND ITS FOREST

The totara is a tall, elegant tree with a straight, branch-free trunk for much of its height. It has a grey or reddish bark, which appears thick, stringy and furrowed. A conifer, the totara's leaves and fruit resemble those of the yew (*Taxus*) species, since they have narrow, needle-like leaves accompanied by bright red, fleshy fruits. There are separate male and female trees and, as they age, the foliage becomes more and more sparse.

Today, where the totara survives, it is regularly found growing in association with the native rimu (*Dacrydium cupressinum*),

matai (*Prumnopitys taxifolia*) and miro (*Prumnopitys ferruginea*), especially on soils that are high in volcanic ash and therefore well drained. The remnants of the great podocarp forests support abundant bird life, such as the kereru, the tui, the fantail, the waxeye and the kaka. There are also populations of the rare New Zealand falcon, the blue duck and North Island robin, and one of the largest remaining populations of the kokako.

Many of the most ancient totara trees and podocarp forests would have been destroyed, had it not been for a series of tree-top protests in 1978. Led by environmentalist Stephen King, a group of protesters managed to prevent the logging of a number of ancient trees, although many had already been felled before the Pureora Forest Reserve was created.

THE MAORIS AND THE TOTARA

Totara timber was greatly favoured by the Maoris and used for a variety of purposes, from everyday house building to ceremonial carvings. The Maoris were extremely skilful in woodmanship: an experienced carver or boat-builder could tell, simply by looking at a totara tree standing in the forest, whether it would be suitable for the purpose he had in mind. The totara was so highly prized that, when a good tree was located, the underbrush would be cleared in advance of its use, as a sign that it was already reserved, or *taunahatia*. The tree might then be left to continue growing for many years before it was finally used.

Sometimes, when a suitable tree for canoe-building was found, a strip of bark was peeled off the trunk. This would induce the tree to rot, making the hollowing-out much easier when the totara was eventually felled. Well-known individuals or groups of totaras were often given names. For example, the tree from which the famous 'Takitimu' canoe was made was known as Te Puwenua.

ABOVE

A view of a remnant of native forest, containing mature totara trees, near Rotorua on the North Island.

In an account written by a European anthropologist, a Mr Barstow, in 1920, it was noted that because canoes were vitally important – whether for war or as a means of procuring food – the tree that was to become the *hiwi*, or hull, was selected from an area that was considered to have good omens. Special chants were used by the *tohunga*, or priest, to improve the good fortune of the finished boat. Specific trees were sometimes even the cause of warfare between two tribes. A special tree might also be left as an heirloom for a son or grandson.

RATA'S WAKA

This is the Maori story of what happened to Rata, who wanted to cut down a totara tree, but had not asked permission from Tane Mahuta – Lord of the Forest:

Long ago, Rata was wandering sadly along the bank of a stream, thinking about his father, who had just died. 'I must bring him home,' thought Rata, 'but how am I going to do that?'

He stared at the trees in the forest and said to himself, 'I need a waka, a canoe big enough to hold many warriors.'

He walked through the forest looking for a suitable tree. 'Miro … rimu … kahikatea … tanekaha … totara. Yes, totara it shall be.'

Early the next morning Rata returned to the forest and chopped down the totara tree. The next day, when he returned, the tree trunk was no longer lying on the ground. Rata stared at the trees around him and, with a start, recognized the totara that he had felled: it was growing tall and proud again, as though it had never been touched. Rata was puzzled and a little fearful.

He took up his axe and began to chop down the totara tree again. The following morning he found it again standing tall and silent. For a third time Rata chopped it down. He shaped it and began to scoop out the inside. When night fell, he left the half-formed canoe and went home.

Later that night he took down his fighting spear and quietly stole back to the forest. As he approached he could hear strange singing and see light shining through the trees. He held his breath and crept closer. Then he stared in amazement. Birds were scurrying backwards and forwards, carrying leaves and twigs in their beaks. Thousands of insects

USES OF THE TOTARA

Totara trees were those most commonly used as timber by the Maoris, most importantly for carving and for making and decorating war canoes, fishing canoes, house-building and *marae*, or ceremonial meeting houses. Strips of bark were used to attach thatching to house frames. Totara is still used for Maori ceremonial objects and for making bowls and other items. The wood is relatively easy to work, but only small amounts of carving can be undertaken at any one time, due to its tendency to split.

LEFT

A detail of the intricate totara carving that adorns the Waitangi Meeting House near Paihia.

were swarming all over the log, replacing chips and filling up the hollow. As he watched, the half-formed canoe disappeared and was replaced by a smooth trunk that glowed red in the light.

Rata could not bear to be hidden any longer. He stood up and stepped into the light. At once the singing stopped and the light went out. Rata was alone. 'Come back,' he whispered. 'I am sorry I cut down the totara tree. Please forgive me. I did not mean to harm it. I just wanted to build a canoe in order to fetch my father.'

He began to lift the heavy trunk. Then all at once he felt it move, turn slowly, lift off the ground and settle on the stump from which he had cut it. Rata put his arms around the tree. As he held onto it, he felt thousands of little legs running over his body and onto the tree trunk. But when the dawn came, Rata was alone. The totara was whole once more. 'I shall never cut down another tree again,' vowed Rata.

'You may,' said a voice close to him. 'But you must ask Tane Mahuta, god of the forest and birds, for permission. He created all these trees and birds for Papatuanuku, the Earth Mother. Ask him when you want to use any of it.'

Rata turned to see who was speaking. There was no one beside him. As he prepared to leave, his heart leapt as he saw a war canoe. 'Mine?' he whispered.

'Yes,' replied the voice. 'Rata's waka.'

In some cases a man might repeat a charm over such a reserved tree in order to preserve it from the elements … lest it be destroyed by Tawhiri-matea [personified form of winds].

ELSDEN BEST, 'THE MAORI CANOE'

BELOW

Part of the carved totara sides of the Ngatokimatawhaorua *canoe at Waitangi.*

British-born Australian botanist J.H. Maiden (1859–1925) wrote in 1894, 'No tree in the brush surpasses it in the quantity of epiphytal vegetation it supports.'

Beneath its mantle of mosses and other vegetation, the trunk of the Antarctic beech has a scaly, porous, dark-red bark, though it turns dark brown when dead and is shed in large, irregular patches. Its twigs and branchlets are covered with a brownish down. An evergreen, the tree has glossy, dark-green leaves that are lance-shaped and finely toothed towards their tips. They feel rigid and leathery to the touch and are brittle in texture. The tree has a compact crown and is seldom without some red or orange-coloured dying leaves. New spring growth, meanwhile, is a deep red. It was this dramatic coloration that gave rise to an earlier name for the tree – red beech – and the name by which its timber has been traded, the Negrohead beech.

Nothofagus moorei is one of a number of related (*Nothofagus*) tree species, commonly referred to as southern beech, that are native to parts of the southern hemisphere. Here they have become important timber trees – in this respect being second only to the eucalypts. Because of their similarity to the beeches of the northern hemisphere, botanists have traditionally described them as part of the tree family to which true beeches (the Fagaceae) belong. Recent research, however, has supported the view that the southern beeches are in fact much more closely related to the birch family (the Betulaceae) and that they should really be placed in a family of their own (the Nothofagaceae).

AN ANCIENT PARTNERSHIP

Over thousands of years the rain forest has come to present a complex, delicate interaction between a vast array of living organisms. The majestic Antarctic beech has become the host for a variety of mosses, ferns and other epiphytic plants, but for one plant it has become almost its only home. This is the beautiful epiphytic orchid *Dendrobium falcorostrum*, one of the largest orchids to be found in the cool temperate rain forests of New South Wales. It was once so common on Antarctic beeches that it was called 'the beech orchid', but it is, like its host, now rare.

LEFT

Between four and twenty snow-white flowers are produced on the beech orchid, displaying yellow and purple markings on the lip.

DISCOVERY OF THE ANTARCTIC BEECH

The Antarctic beech is a survivor from the remote past. Over 200 million years ago the Antarctic continent was covered in luxuriant vegetation and formed part of the super-continent Gondwanaland. Fossil evidence from core samples taken from the ice below Antarctica shows that this vegetation included relatives of the *Nothofagus* species that survive in the southern hemisphere today.

Undoubtedly known to, and held in deep respect by, the Aborigine groups who once made use of the Australian forests in which these trees live, the Antarctic beech has taken its formal botanical name from the British botanist Charles Moore (1820–1905), who was appointed 'government botanist and director of the Botanic Gardens in Sydney' by the Colonial Office in London in 1848.

He set about restoring the scientific character of the gardens, which had become neglected, and, as an avid collector, travelled widely. Moore had a particular interest in the timber trees of Queensland and New South Wales, including the Antarctic beech. This tree had first been 'discovered' by a Mr Carron and a Mr W.A.B. Greaves, on the Upper Clarence River in New South Wales, in 1865. Moore named the Antarctic beech after Mr Carron (*Fagus carronii* Moore), but it subsequently became one of the nineteen species that were named after Moore himself.

At the time that it was first described (the end of the nineteenth century), the trees were much more numerous than they are today, forming dense forests on some of the high mountain slopes in New South Wales. Since it was a particularly slow-growing tree, however, the very hard timber that the Antarctic beech produced became highly sought after. In 1894 Maiden described the wood as follows:

'It is the hardest timber of the brush, and it is also very heavy … There is no doubt that it is a most durable timber … I would look upon it as a valuable timber for culverts and such situations, where it is liable to wet, and I trust that the authorities will give it a fair trial… Large trees throw out burrs, from which depend aerial roots. The timbers of these burrs often yield a beautiful figure.'

The fine and even-textured timber – red when freshly cut, but drying to a pinkish colour – was thereafter extensively used for a number of purposes, including piano construction, cabinet work and soft turnery.

Because of past felling activity, and because regeneration of the young seedlings is so slow, the magnificent Antarctic beech is now rare in the wild. The timber is still traded, however, and has a high commercial value. Fortunately a number of magnificent examples of this ancient tree are now protected in a number of national parks and forest reserves across its natural range.

BELOW
Ancient Antarctic beeches are typically covered in moss and festooned with orchids, ferns and vines.

FIG

Sacred Tree of the Old World

BOTANICAL NAMES
Ficus benghalensis (banyan tree),
Ficus carica (common fig), *Ficus religiosa*
(bodhi fig tree), *Ficus sycomorus* (sycamore fig)

•

DISTRIBUTION
Ficus species are found in all tropical
and some temperate regions.

•

OLDEST KNOWN LIVING SPECIMEN
The bo tree at Anuradhapura, Sri Lanka
is nearly 2,290 years old.

•

RELIGIOUS SIGNIFICANCE
Banyan is sacred to many peoples in India, China and
Southeast Asia; sycamore fig was sacred to the ancient
Egyptians; bodhi tree revered by Buddhists and Hindus.

•

MYTHICAL ASSOCIATIONS
Common fig venerated by the Romans for its
associations with Romulus and Remus; banyan
believed in China and India to be the home
of demons and tree spirits.

FEW GROUPS OF TREES HAVE the religious significance of figs, and few have played such an important part in human history. Truly remarkable fig trees occur, mostly in the tropics, all around the world: some are vast, with canopies measured in entire acres; some are tropical rain-forest giants that strangle their hosts; others are sacred to millions of people; and one individual planted in 288 BC is still thriving today.

There are more than 800 species of fig in the world and they all belong to the same family as the mulberry – the Moraceae. They are found in all tropical and some temperate regions, in countries as diverse as Mexico, China, New Zealand and Namibia.

Fig trees vary enormously in size: while some are only a few feet tall when mature, others can reach heights of more than 147 ft/45 m in tropical rain forests. They tend to be evergreen in tropical regions and deciduous in more temperate climates.

The fig tree features strongly in the religious history and mythology of other parts of the world. The Romans venerated fig trees because, in the story of Romulus and Remus, their cradle became caught on the branches of a fig in a place that was to become Rome. In China, spirits were believed to live in large fig trees, while on the Indian sub-continent sizeable trees were thought to house demons. While the sycamore fig (*Ficus sycomorus*) was, in the Bible lands, 'intimately connected with the rites and mysteries of ancient Nature-worship', as *Plants of the Bible* states, the common fig (*Ficus carica*) was the first plant to be mentioned by name in the Bible, as the source of the 'aprons' of leaves made by Adam and Eve to cover their nakedness. The common fig is referred to no fewer than fifty-seven times in the Bible and is generally synonymous with self-sufficiency.

The fig tree, not that for fruit renowned,
But such as at this day, to Indians known
In Malabar of Deccan spreads her arms,
Branching so broad and long that in the ground
The bended twigs take root and daughters grow
About the mother tree.

JOHN MILTON, 'PARADISE LOST', 1667

THE BANYAN – CROWN OF CROWNS

The banyan tree (*Ficus benghalensis*) is sacred to many peoples across the Indian sub-continent, the Himalayas, China and many parts of Southeast Asia. It is also one of the world's great trees, and individuals can grow to an extraordinary size. So great is the spreading canopy of the banyan that legend has it that Alexander the Great (356–323 BC) and his entire army sheltered under a single tree.

The most famous banyan tree, in terms of size, is located in the Calcutta Botanic Garden in India. It started life in the canopy of a date-palm growing in the botanic garden just 200 years ago. From these humble beginnings it has grown into one of the world's largest-canopied trees. Today, its crown has an average diameter of more than 430 ft/ 131 m, supported by more than 1,775 prop-roots, providing shade for more than 20,000 people. However, there are a number of banyan trees that are considerably older, and other examples of greater size. Perhaps the most remarkable banyan fig is the one growing on the banks of the Nebudda River, east of Bombay. This tree has a truly colossal canopy, measuring an astounding 637 ft/194 m in diameter, which is supported by 320 main stems and more than 3,000 smaller ones. It is virtually a one-tree forest.

There is a long history of belief in Asia that demons and spirits inhabit large trees, and banyan trees feature in many traditional stories. One Indian legend refers to a large banyan tree, which was the home of a number of tree spirits, who were said to wring the neck of anyone who approached at night. In China, tree spirits were believed to manifest themselves as bulls, serpents and a number of other creatures. One of the most revered trees in China is the great Green Banyan of Ching.

Banyan trees were known to people in the Middle East in biblical times. Some scholars propose that the Tree of Life growing in the centre of the Garden of Eden was a banyan. This theory is supported by the view that only the large, broad leaves of this particular tree would have sufficed for sewing together to make appropriate coverings.

A carving of Buddha's head set into the trunk of a sacred fig tree in Thailand.

TREE OF KNOWLEDGE

Ficus religiosa is known by a variety of names, most commonly bodhi and bo. It is one of the most sacred trees in India, Sri Lanka and Nepal, where it is venerated by both Hindus and Buddhists. The name bodhi can be translated as 'tree of knowledge'. Buddhists regard the bodhi as the personification of Buddha, since he is said to have attained enlightenment beneath such a tree at Bodh Gaya in northeast India, over 2,600 years ago. This event is often depicted in images of Buddha under a large, spreading bodhi

A large sycamore fig growing in Kruger National

Park, South Africa (right). The small, heart-shaped leaves

of the bo tree (below) are sometimes used as canvases for

miniature religious paintings.

A large, spreading banyan tree in Rajasthan,

India, displaying the tangle of branches and aerial

roots that are typical of this species.

tree, with demons attacking him on one side and vanquished demons escaping on the other. According to ancient tradition, the original bodhi tree at Bodh Gaya was nurtured by the earth goddess and, at the very moment of Buddha's enlightenment, all the flowering trees in the world burst into flower and became heavy with fruit.

The bo tree is also revered by Hindus, who have a strong religious objection to cutting it down. In the Hindu religion, Vishnu (the second member of the Hindu trinity) is said to have been born under a bo tree and is often depicted sitting on its heart-shaped leaves. The bo tree is often planted in the grounds of temples and, of all the sacred trees of India, it is the most widely worshipped.

Ficus religiosa is a large, fast-growing, deciduous tree, which – unlike many other fig species – does not have aerial roots. It is not a strangler, but splits its host tree as it grows. The trunk is fluted and covered in a smooth grey bark. It has large heart-shaped leaves that taper to a point and these are set on long, slender stalks, causing the foliage to shimmer in the lightest of breezes.

The most famous sacred bo tree in Sri Lanka is located in Anuradhapura, once the capital of the ancient kingdom of Ceylon; it is the oldest tree in the world with a known planting date. It is said that this fig grew from a branch taken from the original bo tree under which Buddha received enlightenment, which was sent to King Tissa in 288 BC. The king planted it and prophesied that it would thrive for ever. Other bo trees found in temple gardens across Sri Lanka are all thought to be cuttings from the famous bo tree of Anuradhapura.

TREE OF LIFE AND AFTER-LIFE

The sycamore fig (*Ficus sycomorus*) is a robust, wide-spreading, semi-evergreen tree found in an area stretching from the Middle East, north and central Africa as far south as KwaZulu Natal in southern Africa. Unlike the banyan, the sycamore fig does not spread out laterally with the aid of aerial roots. Instead, its main trunk, clad in pale-brown, papery bark, divides into numerous spreading branches close to the ground. It is not a tall tree, however, typically growing to just 30–40 ft/9–12 m tall, and large specimens have a spreading canopy of only about 120 ft/36 m in diameter. The largest sycamore fig, and probably the oldest, stands in the Kruger National Park in South Africa. In comparison with other trees of known age, this fig must be well over 1,000 years old.

The sycamore fig was particularly important to the ancient Egyptians, who revered impressive trees. It grew abundantly and was considered to be one of the two most sacred trees of ancient Egypt. As such, it often featured in Egyptian sculptures and was occasionally was represented as the 'Tree of Life'. A mythical sycamore fig even stood on the path to the after-life, supplying food and drink to the souls of the dead on their journey to the Otherworld.

CEDAR

Tree of the Gods

BOTANICAL NAMES
Cedrus libani (cedar of Lebanon), *Cedrus brevifolia*
(sometimes known as cedar of Cyprus), *Cedrus atlantica*
(Atlas or Algerian cedar), *Cedrus deodara* (deodar)

•

DISTRIBUTION
Cedar of Lebanon: Lebanon, Syria and Taurus
Mountains, Turkey; *Cedrus brevifolia*: western Troodos
Mountains, Cyprus; Atlas or Algerian cedar: Atlas
Mountains, Algeria and Morocco; deodar: western
Himalayas, from northern Pakistan and Afghanistan
through Kashmir to western Nepal.

•

OLDEST KNOWN LIVING SPECIMEN
Cedar of Lebanon: ancient grove on slopes of Mount
Lebanon, some believed to be around 1,000 years; deodar
and Atlas cedar: oldest verifiable around 600 years.

•

RELIGIOUS SIGNIFICANCE
The cedar of Lebanon was revered by ancient peoples
of the Holy Land; the deodar is regarded as the
'tree of the gods' by Hindus in India.

•

CONSERVATION STATUS
Cedar of Lebanon: classified in the World List of
Threatened Trees as 'heavily threatened' in Lebanon and
'extremely restricted' in Syria; *Cedrus brevifolia*:
classified globally as 'vulnerable'.

TO MANY PEOPLE THE CEDARS REIGN supreme among the conifers, unequalled by any others for their majestic form and their aura of great antiquity. Whether at home, among the mountains of their native lands, or gracing the lawns of distinguished country houses, the cedars stand out, seemingly timeless and immortal.

Many different conifers, with dark, scented wood, have been called 'cedars' in an attempt to classify them. In North America we find, among others, the western and eastern red cedars, the incense and Alaskan cedars. In the Far East, meanwhile, the Chinese cedar and Japanese red cedar are two more species with misleading common names. There are, in fact, only four true cedars. Three of these are native to the Mediterranean region, while the fourth comes from the western Himalayas.

As its name suggests, the cedar of Lebanon (*Cedrus libani*) is indigenous to Lebanon, but also to Syria and the Taurus Mountains of Turkey. *Cedrus brevifolia* is found only on the island of Cyprus, where it has a very restricted habitat — a few valleys on the western side of the Troodos Mountains. The Atlas cedar (*Cedrus atlantica*) is a native tree of the Atlas Mountains in Algeria and Morocco, while the deodar (*Cedrus deodara*) grows naturally in the Himalayan region stretching from Pakistan and Afghanistan across northern India to western Nepal.

All these cedars are closely related, so much so that the botanist and explorer Sir Joseph Hooker (1817–1911), who was Director of the Royal Botanic Gardens at Kew from 1865 to 1885, thought that they should all be classified together as one species. Still, today, some botanists believe that the cedar found in Cyprus is only a geographical variation of the cedar of Lebanon. The main difference between the two species is the size of the needles: those of *Cedrus brevifolia*, as its name suggests, being slightly smaller than those of its neighbour on the mainland. In other respects the trees are very similar.

TREES OF THE LORD

Cedars are the trees that are most often mentioned in the Bible, and most of these references are to the famous and much celebrated cedars of Lebanon, known in that country simply as *al Arz* (the cedars), or *al Arz ar Rab* (the cedars of the Lord). It is not difficult to see why the peoples of the Bible lands, including the Israelites, should have held them in such high esteem and regarded them with reverence: cedars would

OPPOSITE

Magnificent cedar of Lebanon forests such as this once stretched from southern Lebanon to the Taurus Mountains in Turkey.

RIGHT AND BELOW

*One of the oldest cedars of Lebanon (right) in
the grove known as the 'cedars of the Lord', near Bcharré,
on the slopes of the Mount Lebanon range. The distinctive
egg-shaped cones of the cedars (below) sit upright on
the horizontal branches.*

ABOVE

*The best examples of Cedrus brevifolia
are to be found in 'Cedar Valley' in the Troodos
Mountains of Cyprus.*

certainly have been the most massive and noblest trees with which they were acquainted and amongst the longest-lived. In the Bible cedars are frequently used as symbols of might, power and dignity; of grandeur, prowess and glory; and of beauty and fruitfulness. In the Song of Songs, cedars are used to help evoke a fitting image of Christ himself: 'his countenance is as Lebanon, excellent as the cedars' (Song of Solomon 5:15).

An ancient biblical myth tells of an angel who took refuge beneath a massive cedar tree during a terrible storm. After the storm had abated, the angel prayed to God that this tree, whose wood was so fragrant and whose shade was so refreshing, would also in the future bear some fruit that would be useful to the human race. This fruit was the sacred body of Jesus Christ. Another biblical story tells of Seth, the son of Adam, planting a cutting from the 'tree of life' on Adam's grave. This cutting eventually grew into a tree with three branches: one of cypress wood, one of cedar and one of olive. It was from this tree that the cross was made upon which Jesus was crucified.

Some 2,500 miles/4,000 km away to the east, the equally majestic deodar engendered similar feelings among the Hindu peoples of northwest India's Himalayan region. The name deodar is derived from the Sanskrit *devadaru* or *deodaru*, and means literally

> *B*ehold, the Assyrian was a cedar in Lebanon
> *with fair branches, and with a shadowing shroud,*
> *and of an high stature; ... the fir trees were not*
> *like his boughs, and the chestnut trees were not*
> *like his branches; nor any tree in the garden of*
> *God was like unto him in his beauty. I have made*
> *him fair by the multitude of his branches: so that*
> *all the trees of Eden, that were in the garden of*
> *God, envied him.*
>
> THE PROPHET EZEKIEL (31: 3, 8-9)

'tree of the gods'. The Himalayas, whose glaciers are the source of the sacred River Ganges, are said to be the home of the Hindu gods and some of their most sacred shrines are found here. The Indian god Shiva, his wife Parva and Vishnu the Preserver are all believed to live in this breathtakingly beautiful region. The Indian state of Uttar Pradesh, in which extensive deodar forests are still to be found, contains India's highest mountain peaks.

Forming what are often regarded as some of the loveliest of the world's forests, the deodar extends in its full range from parts of northern Pakistan and Afghanistan in the west through Kashmir in India to western Nepal. It grows in areas of the outer Himalayas where the full strength of the monsoon is felt, in the intermediate ranges and valleys, and also in arid zones deep within the Himalayas. The hardy deodar has colonized the middle slopes of some of the highest mountain ranges in the world. Throughout this region this stately tree has long been esteemed, like its cousins in Lebanon and Turkey, and in North Africa, for its vigour and beauty and for the great size and age it can reach.

The Hebrew words for cedar, *erez* or *ahrahzim*, used in the Bible, are derived from an old Arabic term meaning 'firmly rooted and strong tree' and this expression could well be used to describe all the cedar species, especially when they reach maturity. While still young, cedars are roughly pyramidal in shape, but as they mature – after about 100 years – and if given the space, their tops flatten out and the branches take on a characteristic horizontal form, becoming large and wide-spreading. The results are impressive and beautiful, as they 'strike their splendid attitudes, forming black plateaux … spreading a black table against the sky', as Hugh Johnson has noted in his *Encylopedia of Trees*.

Few conifers are as graceful or elegant as the deodar, with its pendulous outer shoots, especially when it is young. Although it may develop the flat, spreading top of the Lebanon and Atlas cedars, it generally grows with a straight trunk, in the form of a slender spire. In the wild, its arched leading shoots assist the deodar to grow up through overhead branches of the forest understorey to become a dominant tree. The graceful pyramidal shape that the tree can maintain into maturity, and its weeping-tipped branches, make it easier to distinguish from other cedars. It also differs from the Lebanon and Atlas cedars by having longer needles, and young twigs that are distinctly more downy. The deodar is often, too, a taller tree than the other cedars, reaching some 250 ft/ 76 m in the wild and a girth of some 45 ft/13.7 m. Like the other cedars, however, the colour of its foliage varies greatly, although it is usually a glaucous green or grey, becoming dark green on older trees.

The majestic cedar of Lebanon tends to grow in coppice formation, sending up several gigantic trunks from the base at ground level, with enormous branches attached. It may reach some 130 ft/39.6 m in height and a diameter of around 13 ft/4 m. According to dendrologist Alan Mitchell (1922–95), the volume of timber contained in an ancient, large-branched, multi-stemmed specimen is comparable to that of 'the best coast redwoods and perhaps the giant sequoia'.

FRAGRANT OILS

The cedars are well known for the fragrant oils contained within their wood, which have been put to many different uses. With its warm, spicy fragrance, the oil that is extracted from the deodar is very popular in India and is used in traditional Ayurvedic medicine to treat fevers and pulmonary and urinary disorders, among other maladies. In modern aromatherapy it is used for dermatitis, hair loss and nervous tension and it is said to 'enhance meditative relaxation and intuitive work and relieve stress'.

LEFT

Oil extracted from the deodar is considered the least toxic of all the cedar oils; however, it too is a natural antiseptic and an effective repellent of ants, moths and other insects.

Growing in the wild, in the country after which they have taken their popular name, some people think that the oldest cedars of Lebanon may be 2,500 years old, although cedar expert Dr Sawsan Khuri believes them to be 'around 1,000 years old'. According to tree enthusiast Thomas Pakenham, the 'gnarled and tormented trees' he encountered in Turkey in 1993, which were reported to be older than those in Lebanon, were 'up to 1,000 years old'. Since the largest trees (in the Lebanon) are hollow, exact calculations of their age are difficult to make. The largest deodars and Atlas cedars may also be around 1,000 years old.

TREES OF BEAUTY, TREES OF UTILITY

It is not just the beauty and longevity of the cedars that singled them out for special attention in antiquity. Their fragrant wood was greatly prized for its remarkable durability, the ease with which it could be worked and the enormous size of the timbers that could be cut from it.

The deodar is the strongest of the conifers native to India and one of the country's most important timber trees. The fragrant oil present in its wood (which turns yellowish-brown after cutting) has given it a special durability and resistance to attack by termites. For these reasons it was sought after in India in ancient times for temple construction. More recently it was extensively used for railway sleepers and as construction timber for beams, flooring, posts, door and window frames, furniture and carved sacred icons, as well as for bridges, vehicle bodies, masts and spars.

The cedar of Lebanon, meanwhile, was also widely utilized over a large geographical area. It was used by the Mesopotamians, whose civilization flourished some 4,000 years before the birth of Christ; by the ancient kings of Assyria (from about 2500 BC); and by the rulers of neighbouring countries, especially for building and embellishing their palaces. Egyptian builders are said to have imported the wood before 3000 BC – some of it for carving figures and for making sarcophagi (mummy cases). The oily nature of the wood meant that it was preferred to other woods because it deterred attack by insects (and perhaps stopped them from disturbing the dead!). Famous sea-faring peoples, including the Phoenicians and Venetians, were also to make extensive use of cedar wood for their navies.

But perhaps the most famous use of cedar of Lebanon wood was for the construction of King Solomon's temple in Jerusalem. The third King of Israel, King Solomon (c. 1015-977 BC) built his temple and royal palaces on a magnificent scale. Other great buildings, as well as 'a chariot of the wood of Lebanon' (Song of Solomon 3:9) were also constructed for this great king. The Bible records that Solomon sent a letter to King Hiram of Tyre (today known as Soûr, a port in southwest Lebanon) requesting him to: 'Do business with me as you did with my father, King David, when you sold him cedar logs for building his palace. I am building a temple to honour the Lord my God… [5: 3-4]'

ABOVE

Cedrus brevifolia displaying the distinctive level branches that are typical of all mature cedars.

In order to do this Solomon sent over 180,000 men to cut down the trees and prepare the timber, to carry the provisions necessary and to oversee the work. In addition, King Hiram supplied thousands of his own men to help in the felling of the trees. It was to take seven years of arduous work to complete the temple and thirteen more to build Solomon's private house. King Solomon also built the 'house of the Forest of Lebanon', the great Porch of Judgement and a house for his favourite wife – largely of cedar wood. Descriptions of the size of the temple alone, which was 88½ ft/27 m long and 29½ ft/9 m wide, and had an entrance room that was 177 ft/54 m high, give a good idea of the enormous quantities of cedar wood that must have been involved: 'the walls, the floor and the ceiling were built of cedar boards, and the inside walls were covered with panels of cedar … the cedar panels were decorated with carvings of gourds and flowers; the whole interior was covered with cedar, so that no stone could be seen.' [I Kings 6:15–18]

It is evident that vast forests of Lebanon cedars once existed, and it is known that they formerly extended in a continuous belt from southern Lebanon to the Taurus Mountains of Turkey. However, the continuous onslaught against them for their timber, over several thousand years, has left them almost completely extinguished.

ANCIENT SURVIVORS

The largest surviving natural forests of Lebanon cedars – some 247,000 acres/100,000 hectares – are now found in the Taurus Mountains of southeast Turkey. In Lebanon, only remnants of the ancient forests remain in a few valleys of the Lebanon Mountain range, by far the largest being the Shouf forest at Barouk. The most famous grove, comprising only some 400 trees, is situated at about 6,200 ft/ 1,890 m, near Bcharré on the slopes of the Mount Lebanon range. The youngest big tree in this grove is said to be about 200 years old, while estimates range from 1,000 to 2,500 years for the dozen or so oldest individuals. Other small cedar forests are also to be found at Tannourine, south of Jabal Aïtou, and north of Jabal Qaraqif.

*T*he righteous shall flourish like the palm-tree; he shall grow like a cedar in Lebanon'.

PSALMS (92:12)

The cedars of Lebanon have been a place of pilgrimage for centuries. In the middle of the most ancient grove a chapel has been constructed, where a celebration known as the Feast of the Cedars is held every August. At this time, an elder of the Maronite Church (a brand of Roman Catholicism practised by a sect of Syrian Christians) blesses the trees and asks God to protect this particular grove.

But the sad decline of the cedars of Lebanon is a source of great concern to many. To make matters worse, the presence of goats over long periods of time, browsing on cedar seedlings, has prevented any useful regeneration of the trees. In the nineteenth century, Queen Victoria (1819–1901) was so moved by the cedars' plight that she paid for a wall to be erected around the most famous grove in order to protect it from goats. Measures were also taken more recently to keep out grazing animals, and it is reported that stands of cedars have now begun to regenerate slowly. A much more recent threat, from a more unexpected quarter, has come from the activity of skiers, whose presence near the town of Bcharré has similarly been damaging the regenerating trees. But, according to Dr Khuri, 'Cedars are very easy to grow from seed and there are a large number of nurseries in Lebanon producing cedar seedlings for reforestation.'

Though also extensively used in the past, and still an important timber tree in India, the deodar has fared rather better than the cedar of Lebanon in terms of survival, and large areas of natural forest still exist. Although they are often found growing amid a mixture of other trees, both broad-leaved and coniferous, deodars are gregarious in habit and often form pure forests.

In Pakistan and the Indian states of Kashmir and Himachal Pradesh a spectacular, but now endangered bird, the western tragopan (a short-tailed pheasant) has been found to live only in the upper reaches of the deodar forests. With its eye-catching plumage (the male's brilliant red neck, wattle and eye patches contrasting with its reddish brown and black feathers, which are speckled with white), this beautiful bird – itself an object of reverence – is a fitting guardian of these 'trees of the gods'.

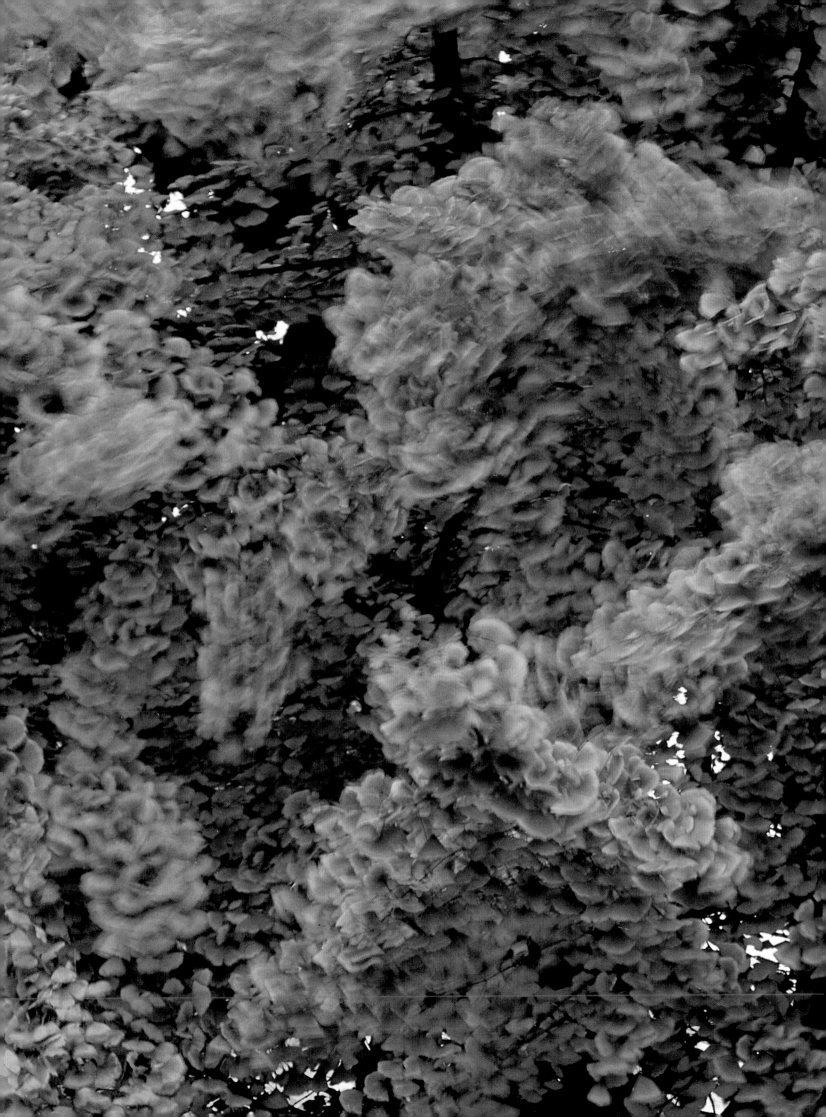

GINKGO

The Dinosaur Tree

BOTANICAL NAME
Ginkgo biloba

•

DISTRIBUTION
Some trees reported to survive in the wild in the
mountains between Zhejiang and Anhui provinces of
China; now widely cultivated throughout
the world as an ornamental.

•

OLDEST KNOWN LIVING SPECIMEN
The tallest ginkgo is in the grounds of the Yon Mun
temple, South Korea: over 200 ft/60 m tall, and
purportedly over 1,100 years old.

•

RELIGIOUS SIGNIFICANCE
Revered by Buddhists in China and Korea,
and by followers of Shinto in Japan, the ginkgo
was planted as a temple tree in antiquity.

•

CONSERVATION STATUS
Classified globally as 'endangered' in the
World List of Threatened Trees.

AN ANCIENT GINKGO TREE IS A SPECTACULAR sight in autumn. The tallest individuals can reach heights of over 200 ft/60 m, and in autumn their leaves turn from apple-green to a brilliant golden yellow. Against a deep-blue Asian sky, this is an awe-inspiring sight and it is not difficult to understand why the tree was revered by Buddhists in antiquity.

The ginkgo is not only a strikingly beautiful tree but also unlike any other tree on earth. It falls into neither of the two main categories of trees – conifer and broad-leaved – but belongs to its very own order (*Ginkgoopsida*), of which it is now the only surviving member. The ginkgo is believed by many scientists to have been the very first tree to evolve, as it has just as many similarities with ferns as it does with trees. It is often called the 'maidenhair tree' by Western botanists, because of the striking resemblance of its leaves to those of the maidenhair fern.

The tree has been given various other names, however. In ancient Chinese it was called *I-cho*, or the 'duck's foot tree', since the shape of its leaves is reminiscent of a duck's webbed foot. It was also known in Chinese as the 'godfather–godson tree', because a tree planted by one generation would begin to produce fruit one or two generations later. However, its most popular name, 'ginkgo', is the Japanese version of the Chinese ideogram which is pronounced *yin-kuo*, meaning 'silver fruit'.

The ginkgo (*Ginkgo biloba*) is a deciduous tree with a graceful grey trunk, which becomes deeply fissured with age. The tree's small leaves soften its shape, without disguising the elegant branches that rise stiffly from the main trunk. Its leaves are fan-shaped and generally have a small cleft in between the two lobes. The ginkgo is so ancient that its system of leaf veins predates those found in any other living tree.

Another unique feature of the ginkgos – which are either male or female – is their method of reproduction. Male trees produce pollen from catkins in order to fertilize the seeds produced by the female trees, but the sperm of the male trees behave in a way reminiscent of ferns – moving on their own to find the female ovary, since the female lacks a pollen tube.

The ginkgo is a true living fossil. It has survived virtually unmodified for the last 200 million years, and it is possible that it was the very first tree to rise from the prehistoric landscape and tower over tree ferns and cycads, the ancient palm-like plants that are native to tropical and sub-tropical regions. Fossil records show that it was once widespread throughout the world, from China to California and from southern Europe to the island of Spitsbergen in the Arctic Circle; 30 million years ago it still formed extensive stands in the London basin.

Until relatively recently, the ginkgo has been able to survive the many great evolutionary changes that have occurred over millions of years, including the attentions of herbivore dinosaurs and a myriad other plant-eating organisms that evolved and later became extinct.

From its dominant position in prehistory, however, the ginkgo has slowly been outdone by other kinds of trees and its range has, over millions of years, gradually shrunk. By the time humans first arrived in Asia about half a million years ago, the ginkgo was only to be found in the Chekiang region of easternmost China and in Sichuan in the far west. Although it has been reported that there are still some trees growing in the mountains between Zhejiang and Anhui provinces, the ginkgo is sometimes regarded as extinct in the wild, and it is only through preservation efforts that so many examples of this relic tree have been saved.

ANCIENT INDIVIDUALS

The tallest and possibly the most spectacular ginkgo today stands in the grounds of Yon Mun temple in South Korea, about 60 miles/96 km north of Seoul. It is a magnificent and very healthy tree, over 200 ft/60 m tall, and displays the ginkgo's classic conical shape. It stands in the grounds of one of the most visited temples in South Korea, set in a dramatic mountain landscape. The trunk is 15 ft/4.5 m thick and the tree is reputed to be 1,100 years old.

TEMPLE GARDENS

The gingko's saviours have been the religious orders of Buddhists in China and Korea and followers of Shinto in Japan, and today the very finest examples are to be found in their temple gardens spread across these three countries. It is not clear exactly why the ginkgos were adopted as temple trees, but their re-emergence as ornamentals was noted as far back as the eighth century.

LEFT

The magnificent 200 ft-/60 m-tall ginkgo at Yon Mun temple in South Korea attracts thousands of visitors every day.

One of the largest gingko trees in South Korea measures 13 m/42.6 ft around the trunk, and is estimated to be at least 800 years old. Local legend records that the tree grew from a stick dropped by a Buddhist priest, who stopped to drink the water. Local people revere this tree as it is said that a huge white snake lives inside. Some also believe that there will be a bumper harvest if the tree's leaves all turn yellow at once.

There are several other giant ginkgos in Korea, but the very oldest trees are believed to exist in China. Although there is no comprehensive list of the most ancient specimens there, one example in Shangdon province has a trunk 16¾ ft/5 m in diameter. Its age is reported to be more than 3,000 years.

Some large trees also occur in Japan, in Shinto temple grounds, but it is believed that these trees were introduced less than 1,000 years ago. And it was in Japan, in 1712, that Westerners saw their first ginkgo; they were then introduced from Japan to Europe in about 1730. Large trees of over 200 years of age can be seen in Britain – the oldest is at the Royal Botanic Gardens, Kew, just outside London, having been transferred there in 1761 from the Duke of Argyll's estate not far away in Twickenham. After a thirty-million-year absence, the ginkgo is once more thriving in the London basin.

ABOVE

Instead of the typical branched veins found in the leaves of other trees, the ginkgo is so ancient in form that its veins fan out from the base and are not interconnected.

DEMAND FOR GINKGO

Ginkgo leaves contain a number of active compounds that are used to treat several medical conditions. Today, ginkgo extracts are worth millions of dollars annually. Their main use in Germany is for the hearing complaint tinnitus, but increasingly herbal preparations that include ginkgo are being used for a whole range of ailments that obtain relief through increased blood flow. These include chilblains, the prevention of and recovery from strokes, Raynauds disease, senile dementia, dizziness and Ménière's disease. To meet the world demand for ginkgo products for the pharmaceutical industry, China is now promoting the cultivation of ginkgos by farmers, and their use as an ornamental plant.

Ginkgo biloba is very hardy and will thrive in a wide range of conditions. It is able to tolerate the polluted air of major cities and is highly resistant to pests and diseases. Horticulturalists have been quick to exploit the natural variations that exist, in order to select and breed many ornamental forms. Since, in autumn time, the falling fruit of the female tree tend to make the area beneath the tree malodorous, it is male trees that are generally planted as ornamentals in large cities.

GINKGO FRUIT

The pinkish-yellow fruits that develop are small, plum-like and hang in pairs. They are, however, notorious for their unpleasant smell. Despite the mildly toxic outer coating of the ginkgo fruit, the seeds inside have long been prized as a food. The whitish or silvery nuts are cracked open to reveal the kernel, which – after roasting – is eaten as a delicacy (much like peanuts or cashews) in the Far East.

Koreans collect the fruits for both food and medicine. Roasted ginkgo kernels are sold on the streets of large cities such as Seoul, while the fruits are used to make remedies for coughs, bladder complaints and asthma. In modern China the fruit are still served at wedding feasts as symbols of fertility, but also because they are said to aid digestion. Other uses include a detergent for washing clothes and a cosmetic made by dissolving the fruit.

OPPOSITE

*Known by locals as 'The Snake Tree',
this ancient ginkgo in South Korea has
many legends attached to it.*

THE MEMORY TREE

In parts of China the ginkgo is known to traditional doctors as 'the memory tree' because of a compound in the leaves that enhances brain activity. One of the oldest Chinese medical texts, dating back to 3000 BC, states that ginkgo leaves 'benefit the brain'. Recent research has shown that a number of terpenes, components of essential oils, which occur naturally in ginkgo leaves, increase arterial blood supply, especially to the brain.

LEFT

*In recent medical trials extracts
from ginkgo leaves were shown to
improve the mental condition of
elderly patients with impaired
mental performance.*

BIBLIOGRAPHY

Arburrow, Y., *The Enchanted Forest* (Capall Bann Publishing, 1993)

Bean, W. J. and eds, *Trees and Shrubs Hardy in the British Isles* (John Murray, 8th edition revised, 1970)

Best, E., 'The Maori Canoe' (*Dominion Museum Bulletin*, no. 7, 1925; reprinted by the Government Printer, Wellington, 1976)

Bierhorst, J., *Mitos Y Leyendas do Los Aztecas* (Editorial Edaf, 1984)

Bosely, D., Jensen, J. and Sinclair, M., *California* (Rough Guides, 1996)

Boyer, M. F., *Tree Talk* (Thames & Hudson, 1996)

Bradt, H., *Guide to Madagascar* (Bradt Publications, UK, 1997)

Bradt, H., Schuurman, D. and Garbutt, N., *Madagascar Wildlife* (Bradt Publications, UK, 1996)

Brown, M., *Dorset: Customs, Curiosities & Country Lores* (Ensign Publications, 1990)

Carder. A., *Forest Giants of the World Past and Present* (Fitzhenry & Whiteside, 1995)

Cavalcante, P. B., *Frutas Comestíveis da Amazônia* (Edições Cejup, 1991)

Chetan, A. and Brueton, D., *The Sacred Yew* (Arkana Penguin Books, 1994)

Collins, M. (ed.), *The Last Rainforests* (Mitchell Beazley, 1995)

Dockrill, A. W., *Australian Indigenous Orchids* (Surrey Beatty & Sons, 1992)

Edlin, H. L. and Nimmo, M. *et al.*, *The Illustrated Encyclopedia of Trees* (Salamander Books, 1978)

Ell, G., *King Kauri* (Bush Press, New Zealand, 1996)

Ell, G., *Kauri, Past and Present* (Bush Press, 1994)

Elliot, W. R. and Jones, D. L., *Encyclopaedia of Australian Plants*, vol. 7 (Lothian Books, 1997)

Elsasser, A. B., *Indians of Sequoia and King's Canyon National Parks* (Sequoia Natural History Association, 1962)

Else, D., Murray, J. and Swaney, D., *Africa – The South* (Lonely Planet, 1997)

Enright, N. J. and Hill, R. S., *Ecology of the Southern Conifers* (Melbourne University Press, 1995)

Escobar, B., Matthews, K. and White, D., 'Pieces of the Puzzle', in *The Garden* (December 1998)

Evelyn, J., *Sylva* (Stobart & Son, facsimile edition, 1979)

Fichtner, C., *Gesegnete Brunnen* (Landsberger Verlagsanstalt, 1992)

Floyd, A. G., *Rainforest Trees of Mainland South-eastern Australia* (Inkata Press, 1989)

Fröhlich, H. J., *Alte Liebenswerte Bäume in Deutschland* (Cornelia Ahlering Verlag, 1989)

Gentry, A. H., *Woody Plants of Northwest South America* (Conservation International, 1996)

Goerss, H., *Unsere Baumveteranen* (Landbuch-Verlag, GmbH, 1981)

Grieve, H., *A Modern Herbal* (Penguin Books, 1984; first published by Jonathan Cape, 1931)

Guppy, N., *Wai-Wai* (John Murray, 1958)

Harden, G. J. (ed.), *Flora of New South Wales,* vol. 1 (Royal Botanic Gardens, Sydney, 1990)

Hart, C., *British Trees in Colour* (Michael Joseph, 1973)

Hayward, B. W., *Kauri Gum and the Gumdiggers* (Bush Press, Auckland, 1989)

Holliday, I., *A Field Guide to Australian Trees* (Landsdowne Publishing, 1995; first published by Rigsby Publishers, 1969)

Hora, B. (ed.), *The Oxford Encyclopedia of Trees of the World* (Oxford University Press, 1981)

Huxley, F., *Affable Savages* (Travel Book Club, n.d.)

Jiménez, V., *El Arbol de El Tule En La Historia* (Codex Editores, 1990)

Johnson, H., *Encyclopedia of Trees* (Mitchell Beazley, 1984)

Johnson, H., *The International Book of Trees* (Mitchell Beazley, 1973)

Jones, W. R., *Yosemite, The Story Behind the Scenery* (KC Publications, 1989)

Jones, W. G., Hill, K. D. and Allen, J. M., '*Wollemia nobilis,* a new living Australian genus and species in the Araucariaceae', in *Telopea*, vol. 6 (2–3), (March–September 1995)

Jordan, M., *Plants of Mystery and Magic* (Blandford, 1997)

Keen, L., *Guide to Lebanon* (Bradt Publications, UK, 1995)

Kelley, M. S., *Congress Trail – Sequoia National Park* (Sequoia Natural History Association, 1978)

Lewington, A., *Plants for People* (Natural History Museum, 1990)

Mabberley, D. J., *The Plant-Book* (Cambridge University Press, 1989)

McCrea, B., Pinchuck, T. and Mthembu-Salter, G., *South Africa, Lesotho & Swaziland* (Rough Guides, 1997)

McIntyre, C., *Namibia,* (Bradt Publications, UK, 1998)

McLaughlan, G., *Insight Guides: New Zealand* (APA Publications (HK), 1995)

Maiden, J. H., *The Forest Flora of New South Wales,* vol. VII (John Spence, Acting Government Printer, 1922)

Manchao, C., *The Origin of Chinese Deities* (Foreign Languages Press, Beijing, 1997)

Margolin, M. (ed.), *The Way We Lived: Californian Indian Stories, Songs and Reminiscences* (Heyday Books, 1993; first published 1991)

Marren, P., *Woodland Heritage* (David & Charles, 1990)

Matus, M., *Los Zapotecas; Binni Záa* (Direcciecas; Binni Záa st published 1991), SonMeninger, E. A., *Fantastic Trees* (Timber Press, 1995)

Milner, J. E., *The Tree Book* (Collins & Brown, 1992)

Milton, J., *Paradise Lost* (ed. Fowler, A.), (Longman, 1971)

Mitchell, A., *Alan Mitchell's Trees of Britain* (HarperCollins, 1996)

Mitchell, A., *A Field Guide to the Trees of Britain and Northern Europe* (William Collins, reprinted 1986)

Moldenke, H,N and A.L., *Plants of the Bible* (Dover Publications, 1986)

Nairn, B., Serle, G. and Ward, R. (section eds), *Australian Dictionary of Biography,* vol. 5 (Melbourne University Press, n.d.)

North, M., 'In Pursuit of the Puzzle-Monkeys in Chili', in *Pall Mall Gazette* (11 March 1885)

Oldfield, S., Lusty, C. and MacKinven, A. (eds), *The World List of Threatened Trees* (World Conservation Press, 1998)

Opie, I., *Dictionary of Superstition* (Oxford, 1989)

Pakenham, T., *Meetings with Remarkable Trees* (Weidenfeld & Nicolson, 1996)

Parmer, E. and Pitman N., *Trees of South Africa* (A. A. Balkema, 1961)

Paterson, J. M., *Tree Wisdom* (Thorsons, 1996)

Pickering, D., *Dictionary of Superstition* (Cassell, 1985)

Porteous, A., *The Lore of the Forest* (Senate, 1996; first published by Allen & Unwin, 1928)

Rackham, O., *Trees and Woodland in the British Landscape* (J. M. Dent, 1976)

Radford, E. and M. A., *Encylopedia of Superstition* (Hutchinson, 1969)

Riley, M., *New Zealand Trees & Ferns* (Viking Sevenseas, 1983)

Rosenblum, M., *Olives, The Life and Lore of a Noble Fruit* (Absolute Press, 1996)

Sahni, K. C., *The Book of Indian Trees* (Bombay Natural History Society/Oxford University Press, 1998)

Salmon, J. T., *The Reed Field Guide to New Zealand Native Trees* (Reed Books, 1996; first published 1986)

Sastri, B. N. (chief ed.), *The Wealth of India* (Delhi, 1950)

Silcock, L. (ed.), *The Rainforests, A Celebration* (Barrie & Jenkins, 1989)

Sisitka, L. *et al., Guide to the Care of Ancient Trees* (English Nature, 1996)

Smart, R., *Trees and Woodlands of Cheshire* (Cheshire Landscape Trust, 1992)

Tree News [periodical], (The Tree Council, Autumn 1996)

Venter, F. and J. A., *Making the Most of Indigenous Trees* (Briza Publications, 1996)

Vickery, R., *Oxford Dictionary of Plant Lore* (Oxford University Press, 1995)

Wallace, A. R., *A Narrative of Travels on the Amazon and Rio Negro* (Ward, Lock, 1890)

Werner, E. T. C., *Myths & Legends of China* (Graham Brash, Singapore, 1984; reprinted 1995)

White, E., *The Flowering of Gondwana* (Princeton University Press, 1990)

White, J., *Estimating the Age of Large and Veteran Trees in Britain* (Information Note: Forestry Commission, November 1998)

Wildwood, C., *The Encyclopedia of Healing Plants* (Piatkus, 1997)

Williamson, R., *The Great Yew Forest* (Macmillan, 1978)

Wilson, E.H., *China: Mother of Gardens* (Benjamin Blom Inc, 1971)

Woodcock, M.W., 'The Auracaria Imbricata or Monkey Puzzle Tree', in *The Tree Lover,* vol. 3 (1941)

Woodward, M. (ed.), *Gerard's Herball* (Bracken Books, 1985)

Yew News [periodical], no. 1 (Conservation Foundation, March 1997)

A number of issues of the following journals were also consulted:

Economic Botany (New York Botanic Garden)

Kew (Royal Botanic Gardens, Kew/Michael Godfrey)

New Scientist (Reed Business Information)

Non-Wood Forest Products (FAO, Rome)

Non-Wood News (FAO, Rome)

Plant Talk (Botanical Information Company)

ANCIENT TREES AND CONSERVATION

This book was designed as a celebration of the world's oldest trees and it is hoped that it will inspire further interest in the magnificent trees and forests that still grace our planet. We have presented, among others, chapters on the mighty redwoods, the giant baobabs and the curious dwarf tree of the Namib Desert, the welwitschia.

However, many of the world's most ancient trees and the environments that support them are under threat. In California, for example, large numbers of ancient coast redwoods, many over 1,000 years old, have been felled during the 1990s. And despite the clamour of warnings and publicity given to the deforestation of the Amazon in recent times, the rate of destruction there has actually accelerated in the last ten years. Even protected species, such as the monkey puzzle of Chile, are being affected, on a number of fronts – for example, by the felling of tree species that grow in association with them, and from attack by a fungus that appears to be spreading due to the indirect effects of global warming. Forests and individual trees worldwide are suffering from more stresses than ever, including atmospheric pollution, overgrazing, droughts, the introduction of exotic species and general clearance on a huge scale. European oaks, for instance, are suffering such levels of disease and defoliation that scientists from many disciplines have come together to work on an EU project to try and reverse the decline.

Ancient trees can perhaps be placed in three separate categories: those in urban settings, those in semi-wild situations and those in wildernesses, such as old-growth forests. Many old trees that are to be found today in urban areas, such as the great limes of Germany, or the tree known as 'El Tule' near Oaxaca in Mexico, tend to be locally famous and enjoy some form of protection. However, those in semi-wild settings are often known only to a few people and many are found on private land, where there is little or no formal protection.

In some cases public pressure can be brought to bear on landowners to protect their trees, as happened when a number of the ancient oaks (known as 'dodders') in Windsor Great Park began to be felled. Public pressure also forced the US government to purchase the last large area of privately owned old-growth coast-redwood forest from a logging company in 1999. Many of the world's tree veterans, however, exist in isolated locations, often within remnants of ancient forest, and are effectively invisible to the world outside. Although ancient trees are just one of the myriad components that make up a living forest ecosystem, it is becoming increasingly apparent that they are crucial to its proper functioning.

Forests perform a number of vital local and global environmental services: for example, regulating climates and ameliorating the effects of global warming by 'locking up' carbon dioxide (one of the greenhouse gases). Recent research has shown that ancient trees within old-growth forests contain a significant proportion of the forest's stored carbon. To fell such trees, therefore, has a far greater effect on the global climate than felling mature trees in relatively modern plantations. They are also important in the maintenance of biodiversity, because of the large number of other species they support.

WWF 'FORESTS FOR LIFE' CAMPAIGN

Over the last ten years we have had the privilege of working in many of the world's forests, often as consultants to WWF. It was on such assignments, and particularly carrying out work related to the Forests for Life Campaign, that the idea for this book was born. As WWF itself states:

'Forests are vitally important for all life on earth. Forests and woodlands not only provide wood, medicines and other valuable products, but they also purify the air we breathe, help combat the greenhouse effect, provide a livelihood for indigenous people and are home to countless species of plants and animals.

But forests are disappearing at an alarming rate. Once distributed over half the earth, forests now cover only one-third of the land surface. Recognizing the importance of halting this cycle of destruction, WWF has made forests one of its priorities for action.

Through the work of its International Forest Programme and Forests for Life Campaign, WWF is committed to halting and reversing this continuing loss and degradation by the year 2000. Together with WWF national offices around the world, WWF is running more than 300 forest projects in over 65 countries.

The Forests for Life Campaign promotes the establishment and practical realization of an ecologically representative network of protected areas covering at least ten per cent of each of the world's forest types by the end of the year 2000. Only six per cent of the world's forests are currently in protected areas. The independent certification of at least 25 million hectares of well-managed forests by June 2001 focusing on key timber producing countries. More than 17 million hectares have been certified to date.'

WWF website: http:\\www.panda.org/forest4life

OTHER ANCIENT TREE SPECIES

It was never the intention of *Ancient Trees* to be an encyclopaedic book of the world's longest-lived trees. However, in the course of our research we have compiled a large list, which has now grown to almost 100 species. As a consequence there are many species of tree that we would have liked to include, but time and space prohibited this. However, we feel that the following deserve to be mentioned:

The alerce (*Fitzroya cupressoides*) is sometimes referred to as the giant redwood of South America, and it is known to live to more than 3,000 years old. In the temperate rain forests of south-central Chile these colossal trees, whose trunks almost reach the size of those of the largest giant redwoods, once formed extensive stands. These forests, however, have been massively exploited and, although forests of young trees are regenerating, the giant ancient trees have been harvested to virtual extinction. One of the few surviving giants now has its own guard!

The Algerian cypress (*Cupressus dupresiana*) is perhaps the most threatened of all the ancient tree species. The last remaining stand of trees, some of which are more than 1,000 years old, number only 150.

Some experts believe that the world's oldest tree may be a huon pine (*Dacrydium franklinii*) living in the forests of southwest Tasmania. Trees have already been discovered that are more than 3,000 years old, and in some trees the tree rings are so tightly packed that there may be more than 1,000 of them in a trunk that measures just 12 in/30 cm across. Once heavily exploited, the oldest huon pines are now believed to reside mostly in National Parks.

Another ancient tree that is also found in the Tasmanian wilderness is the king billy pine (*Athrotaxis selaginoides*). This tree is known to live to well over 1,000 years and now also enjoys protection within National Parks.

Rimu (*Dacrydium cupressinum*) is found on both islands of New Zealand. It is a podocarp and a survivor from the forest that once clothed the super-continent of Gondwanaland. Known to live to 1,160 years old, these trees are still being harvested in the South Island of New Zealand, although the trunks are cut individually and then removed by helicopter to cause the minimum disturbance.

There are various juniper (*Juniperus*) species around the world that also attain very great ages. These ancient trees range in size from only a few feet tall in Turkey to towering giants in the Sierra Nevada of California. They are often found in very harsh environments, such as the arid and eroded hills of the Middle East and the White Mountains in California, where they grow alongside the bristlecone pines.

The Japanese cedar (*Cryptomeria japonica*) is another possible candidate for the longest-lived tree species. One unconfirmed report indicated that a stump had been found with up to 7,000 rings.

The western red cedar (*Thuja plicata*), a native of the cool temperate rain forests of North America's Pacific seaboard, has been an important tree to the Tlingit and other indigenous peoples for thousands of years. Known to live to over 1,000 years and to reach heights of more than 200 ft/61 m, this tree has been used in house- and boat-building for its timber, and for totem poles.

INDEX

Numbers in *italics* refer to illustrations.

ACKNOWLEDGEMENTS

Very many people have helped us in many different ways to undertake the research and photography for this book, and we are greatly indebted to them all.

First of all, we must thank Francis Sullivan and Alison Lucas of WWF. They not only provided funding for the initial research trip to Australia and New Zealand, but had faith in this project from the start.

Many members of the WWF staff around the world assisted us, and special thanks are due to Dr Steve Howard and Peter Newborn (WWF UK). We would also like to thank Sandra Charity, and Dr Alan Hamilton (WWF UK), Chris Elliott (WWF International), Ugis Rotsberg (WWF Latvia), Dr Lei (WWF China), and Michael Rae (WWF Australia).

The help given to us by members of staff of The Royal Botanic Gardens, Kew, is also greatly appreciated; in particular Dr Aljos Farjon and Barbara Lowry who were most generous with their time and advice, Jeffrey Wood, Dr Pat Griggs, Dr Geoffrey Kite, Dr Stuart Henchie, Anne Marshall and Helen Sanderson. Many thanks are also due to Laura Ponsonby (formerly of Kew).

We are very grateful for the expert advice and statistical information given to us by David Alderman and Pamela Stevenson of the Tree Register of the British Isles, and also by distinguished dendrologist John White, TROBI's technical adviser. Information from Jeroen Pater in Holland is also much appreciated. We were greatly assisted and inspired also by the work of Canadian botanist Al Carder. Other individuals we must thank include Dr Sawsan Khuri (University of Reading), Anna Hallett (Royal Botanic Gardens, Sydney), Niro Higuchi (Instituto Nacional de Pesquisas da Amazonia, Manaus), Dr Jeffrey Chambers (University of California, Santa Barbara), Dr Martin Gardner (Edinburgh Botanic Garden), Mark Atterton and Laura Battlebury (World Conservation Monitoring Centre), Libby Simon (Conservation Foundation), Rachel Thackray (Thackray Forrester Communications), Dr Tim Synott (Forest Stewardship Council, Oaxaca), Garth Nikles (Queensland Forest Research Institute), Dr Antonio Lara (Universidad Austral, Chile), Patrick Curry (Friends of the Ankerwyke Yew), Ian Aldred (Cheshire County Council), John Gittens (Cheshire Landscape Trust), Brian Ayres (Archaeology and Environment Department, Norfolk County Council), Sonia Williams (Crawley Library), Nick Lawrence (Dorchester Reference Library), and Herr Hannich (Schenklengsfeld Town Council). Other organizations that helped us include the Royal Society for the Protection of Birds, World Pheasant Association, Goethe Institute, German National Tourist Office and the Comité Nacional pro Defensa de la Fauna y Flora (Codeff), Chile.

We also received vital practical support from Peter and Edwina Parker and Peggy Hart, and the help of several friends was outstanding throughout, particularly that of the ever-patient Terry Jenkins, Andy Cross (a very fine botanist), Peter Salbert (in Germany), and Yeo Dong Wan and Juin (in Korea), all of whom went to great lengths to help us. We must also thank our great friends Bryan and Cherry Alexander, who were always ready to offer advice and help throughout the project.

Thanks are also due to the following individuals: Anand Chetan, John Gilchrist, Jack Weber, Richard Dodge, Reynaldo and Alfredo Meliñir, Reynaldo Mariqueo, Stephen King, Richard Head, Ray Oddi, Wilma Rittershausen, Lucinda Lachlin, Sheila Morrissey, Tom and Benita Denny, Emma Parker, Richard Parker, Charles and Debbie Parker, Peter Vinson, Merilyn Thorrold, Mr and Mrs A. Blanchard, and Peter Abounader. Martin Bracey, Jesus Ortega, Stephen and Wendy Knight, Victoria Wiles and Emma Adamou all helped make life bearable for us and our children during the writing of this book, and we thank them kindly. We are also grateful to Tony Lewington for his constant encouragement.

Finally, we would like to thank Sarah Hoggett and Katie Bent (at Collins & Brown) and Mandy Greenfield, whose hard work and enthusiasm are greatly appreciated.

While acknowledging the help that so many individuals and organizations have given us, we must also point out that any mistakes or errors remain entirely our own.

The Publishers would like to extend their grateful thanks to Mandy Greenfield, Liz Cowen and Vicki Robinson for all their help.

PICTURE CREDITS